My Son Killed Himself

From Tragedy to Hope

Jessica Varian

7710-T Cherry Park Drive, Suite 224, Houston, TX 77095

The views expressed in this book are the authors and do not necessarily reflect those of the publisher.

Published in the United States of America.

eBook: 978-1-943848-33-1

Softcover: 978-1-365-76721-0

Hardcover: 978-1-943848-66-9

Psalm 34:18

The LORD *is close to the brokenhearted;*
he rescues those whose spirits are crushed.

CONTENTS

ACKNOWLEDGEMENTS

Above all, thank you God, my Lord and Savior Jesus Christ. You are my refuge, my place of safety, my God and the One in whom I can trust. As my "Daddy" in Heaven, you equipped me with the power and strength of Your Spirit to write the pages of this book. You gave me the fortitude to write in the midst of utter devastation and brokenness of heart. You are faithful, merciful, marvelous, and full of love and compassion in all of your ways. I love you, Jesus.

Thank you Jeffrey, my son, for helping and encouraging me throughout this project. I know by the grace and power of God you are becoming the man of God we have prayed for. You know how much I love you and you can count on me as long as I have breath. I am so proud of you.

Thank you mom and dad. You taught me to never give up on life and to never quit believing and trusting in God. You have shown me living proof on how to keep the faith and to forgive no matter how much it hurts. I am blessed by having you as my parents. I love you both.

I thank all of my friends and in-laws who were with me, by my side during those horrific hours. The love and support each of you provided me has been such a source of encouragement and strength.

Thank you Pastor John and Jean Counts, my spiritual parents. You taught me the Word of God, how to exercise the gifts of the Holy Spirit and the power of worshipping the living God. Everything you planted in me prepared me for the darkest days of my life. Pastor Counts is no longer with us but the impact he had on our entire family was so profound it will last a lifetime. We will love him always. We love you Pastor Jean.

Thank you, Dr. Red* (name changed). You have been a pillar and mentor in my life for well over 17 years. You were always there to guide and oversee me even during the worst moments of my life and you never failed me. You invested countless hours of time and energy into both me and Jorge, all for our best outcome. Thank you for your support when I expressed to you that I needed to write this book as you read each chapter with me seeing them through until completion.

Thalia Ruiz, I am so grateful that you came into my life at the precise moment when I doubted whether to publish this book or not. You spoke to my heart and were a vessel for the Lord, so that the purposes of God would be accomplished. You are a soldier for the Kingdom and I am blessed to know you and have you as a friend.

Thank you, Eddie Smith with Worldwide Publishing Group, without whose support this book would not be possible.

Lastly, thank you George, my beloved husband. You have been so wonderful and strong in faith. You have shown me to believe in the Word of God in the midst of the storm, to stand firm in faith never relenting. You have demonstrated to never give an inch to the enemy and never surrender my hope.

Acknowledgements

You are my best friend and the love of my life. Thank you for dedicating hours that became days, days that became weeks, and weeks that became months to make sure this book could be all that it could be. Without your skills, knowledge, patience, and vision this book would never have reached its purpose and potential. You have been my advisor, editor, producer, theologian, consultant, focus, researcher and partner in the plan and purpose of God for this project. To you my loving, sweet and caring soul; to you my husband I join in giving all glory to God.

My Son Killed Himself

DEDICATION

I dedicate this book in memory of my eldest and dearly loved son, Jorge Roberto. I wish life would have been so very different for both of us. We would have never conceived it would have unfolded the way it did. If only I could have stopped his pain, internal struggles, and the tragic events that he experienced. Oh, how I dream of going back and rescuing him from it all. I know there is nothing I can rescue him from at this point as God Himself has rescued him from his pain. I am greatly relieved, knowing that he no longer has need of anything! Yet my heart cries out. It cries out—

Forgive me my son for failing you. I will treasure you in my heart and in my memories forever. You changed my life in every way my son. I will never forget you!

As I review the pages of your life's story, I'm convinced that your death wasn't a loss nor was it in vain. On the contrary, your life has left us strengthened with a message of faith, hope and love. You changed our lives immeasurably, forever in so many ways. Your amazing ability to forgive so many of those who harmed you and your unwavering love towards us will never be forgotten. Your smile, oh that smile, which could light up the night's sky. Your mere presence would bring us happiness the moment you would come near. You also showed us the consequences of taking wrong paths. We have learned from your mistakes and from the erroneous things you did.

Through the story of your life, we saw the enlightened path that God creates for each of us to follow. We have learned from your constant battles. We saw the consequences of trying to live a life without Christ, in contrast we experienced the glorious results of one's life where Jesus becomes Lord to reign supreme. First hand we saw the goodness of God and the reality that Jesus Christ is the only answer to life's problems.

My son, your life was like a blink of an eye compared to all of eternity. The struggles you faced and the lessons you learned are so common to many in this world and are now your gift to us because they were not in vain. Though it wasn't your intent, your life taught us so much in such a short time. It instructed us to stay away from evil and sin of every shape and form because it will only bring destruction, pain, suffering, loss, and death.

It is my honor and my gift to you, my son, to tell you that your life was not wasted. Your life was meaningful, relevant and fervently reminds us of the important things in life; things like family, unity, love, faith, and the importance of saying "no." We are reminded to keep our hearts filled with forgiveness; to remain alert, to walk circumspectly, leaving nothing for the enemy to steal from us. We know now to give our all to Christ Jesus, the only One who loves us and was willing to give His life to save us from eternal damnation. He gives us His Spirit, peace, power, strength, and wisdom so we can live without regret and to die without fear. **Thank you, Jorge. "Tu mamá te ama." (Your mother loves you).**

Chapter One
HE'S GONE

"He's gone! He's gone! Jorge is gone! He went to Heaven!" exclaimed the frantic caller late one Friday afternoon in March 2011. Suddenly, everything else faded away into a blur. I could not fully comprehend what I had just heard, yet somehow I knew what it meant. My heart suddenly gripped with the most excruciating and unspeakable pain, as though a knife had fiercely stabbed my heart. The pain, so pulsating and severe; I was unable to function, nearly catatonic for the next three days.

A Week Before

I was making final preparations for a surgical procedure I was to have at the hospital when I learned that my husband (George) and my son (Jorge) had experienced a disagreement over something. I was not fully aware of the nature of the disagreement, though I knew it was such that they were refusing to speak with one another. Immediately, I recognized that the disagreement between them was orchestrated by the master of division and destruction, Satan, the enemy of all mankind. I asked two of my closest friends and spiritual warriors to join me in a time of powerful prayer. I prayed—

"I thank you Heavenly Father for the blood of your only Son Jesus Christ, who has redeemed

13

us and given us access to you. By the power of your Holy Spirit, I proclaim to darkness, demons, principalities and dominions in the highest places, "NO MORE!" You have no authority to disrupt my life or the life of my son Jorge and my family this way. We are sons and daughters of God Almighty and the blood of Jesus covers us. I command you to back off! Back off! I say again, back off! You have no right! I say to you at this moment RELEASE MY FAMILY and MY SON! You cannot trespass on what has already been purchased by the Blood of Christ Jesus. He paid the price for our freedom and by virtue of what He did on the cross gives us peace. I will not allow you to destroy and disrupt my family. I am a child of God, and I am in Him (Jesus) and He (Jesus) is in me. You are not allowed to destroy my family. In the Name of Jesus, I have authority over you, and I command you to stop all lies, divisions and dissensions right now in my Lord Jesus Christ. You have no authority over our lives, Jorge belongs to God because of His covenant with me and is covered by the Blood of Jesus. I command you to leave now!" (This prayer was based on the following Scriptures: Mark 16:17; John 12-13; Ephesians 1:17-22, 6:10-17; and Hebrews 10:19-21.)

I knew in my spirit that this disagreement was the latest scheme of Satan to destroy our hopes and dreams, tear us down, divide us, and cause us pain. He (Satan) is a liar and deceiver, always finding ways to hurt us and blame the Lord in Heaven for all the pain he has caused. (1 Peter 5:8)

Later, that evening when I arrived home, I spoke with Jorge and asked him if he was going to come to the hospital and keep my husband company while I was in surgery. He told me he would see me at home when I returned from the hospital. He felt, after their disagreement, it would be better if he allowed some time to pass.

Early the next morning as I left for the hospital, I still hoped he would reconsider and come with me. He didn't. After my surgery, I kept my cell phone in hand, waiting for his call. Even in my delirium, I knew he wasn't there. Suddenly my phone rang. It was Jorge. He asked me how I was doing. I told him that I was in a lot of pain. He told me that he loved me with all his heart. I repeatedly told him how much I loved him. Later that night he sent me a sweet text message that read "Goodnight Mama, I love you."

As a new day was breaking so did the excitement of going home. Jorge must have been excited too, because he called me many times that morning, asking me how I was feeling. With each phone call and text message we exchanged, we told each other how much we loved each other. Our excitement didn't last, however, because the doctor decided to keep me at the hospital for another day.

When I found out I wasn't going home as planned, I asked Jorge if he was going to come visit me at the hospital. He told me that he had a terrible sore throat, and he said he needed to go to the doctor first to be sure that he wasn't contagious. I told him to call me after his doctor's appointment to tell me what the doctor said, and to see how he was feeling. Later that day he called me and told me that he had strep throat. The doctor advised him not to see me until he had antibiotics in his system for at least three days.

The next morning I awoke with great anticipation of leaving the hospital. Despite the fact, I was barely able to walk and in a terrible amount of pain, I left the hospital and went home.

"Finally, home at last!" I proclaimed.

I spent the next two days in bed in such pain I even dreaded the thought of getting up to walk to the bathroom. Thankfully, my husband had taken the week off from work to care for me. As usual, I was talking to Jorge constantly, and we were, always concerned with how the other was doing, asking incessantly.

Monday morning came, and I called Jorge around 9:30 a.m. and asked him if he was coming to see me. He told me "No, because...", and he gave me an excuse. "You promised!" I insisted. In my heart I knew Jorge wanted to come see me, but something more was going on. He felt trapped in his problems, and he was also very conflicted about the words he had exchanged with my husband the day before my surgery.

Finally, he told me, "Okay Mom, I am coming right now. I'm on my way, okay?" I was relieved to know I would see my son after what had seemed like many long days.

He Finally Arrived

About an hour later, he finally arrived. I was surprised to see him wearing a T-shirt and jogging pants that looked like pajamas. He was disheveled and visibly distressed. No sooner than we said hello and exchanged a hug and kiss, his eyes moved to the kitchen where he spotted the bottle of Hydrocodone I was taking for pain. He told me that the strength prescribed by my doctor was inadequate for the level of pain I was experiencing. According to him, I needed something stronger, and he proceeded to tell me the exact strength I should be taking (10-650 mg). Within a few minutes, he was already calling my doctor's office and asking for a higher dosage of the prescription, saying that I was requesting due to the pain. I was very upset. I kept telling him to hang-up, but he ignored me and continued talking. Then I heard him give the phone number to his drugstore that was nearest to his home address to pick up the prescription.

I got very angry with him when he did this; I felt it was disrespectful. In my heart, I knew what he had just done since he had just stopped taking Hydrocodone two weeks prior after a nearly nine-month addiction.

I repeatedly told him "No, no, I don't need anything else, Jorge." I told him that I was going to call the doctor and cancel the order that he requested. I told him I wasn't going to pick up that prescription because I didn't need it. But I was in so much pain that I could barely move around. It was all I could do to stand, so I started to go back to the bed on my own.

As I started to walk to my bedroom, I could hear him in the kitchen opening drawers. I asked what he was doing, and he said he was looking for a wine bottle opener that he knew I used many times while cooking. In great pain I didn't pay any attention to what he was doing or saying as I struggled to get in bed to lie down. When I walked into the bedroom, I realized he had two glasses of white wine in his hands, one for him and one for me. He handed me the glass of wine and said, "Take it, Mom, it will make you feel better." I said, "Jorge you are crazy! How am I going to drink alcohol when I am taking pain pills? Not to mention, why are you drinking this early in the morning?" He put the glass of wine on the table, helped me to get into the bed, and then got into bed with me.

I will never forget when he put his head on my shoulder and told me "Mom, every cell of my body loves you." I will hold those words tight for the rest of my life. He also said, "Mom, now I understand; now I can see clearly what the drugs did to me... now I know all the things they took from me." I felt the pain and regret in his body. Everything within him was shaken by the awareness of this truth which made me utterly sad. My son was a very clean person, but I noticed that he had not taken a bath for days. I remember the smell of his hair as he put his head on my shoulder. It was that waxy smell one gets when they haven't washed their hair for a while. He began to share with me that he couldn't bear the pain of knowing that his "Mami" (my grandmother) had died. Though she had died many years before the reality of it all had finally set in. Telling me that even though he was completely off of Hydrocodone for two full weeks, the memory of her was haunting him. He could no longer suppress the memories and pain with drugs, alcohol or pain pills. He was suddenly awakened to the reality that she was "gone" and he couldn't bear the pain of knowing it. Later in this book you will learn about Jorge's relationship with his Mami, which was central in his life.

At that moment, my husband came home. Jorge sat on the edge of the bed and said to me, "I have to talk to George." He left the bedroom and met my husband at the door as he was coming in. They both went into my husband's home office and closed the doors. After a few minutes, I managed to get up to join them, but I heard them in deep conversation. I knew that it was good for Jorge to talk to my husband, so I climbed back into bed. Due to the pain medication that I was taking, I fell asleep. I awoke a couple of times, heard George and Jorge still talking, then fell back asleep again. When I fully woke up, I was shocked to realize that 2 ½ hours had passed.

Eventually, Jorge came to my room and told me that he had to go. I got up and followed him to the front door asking him why he wasn't going to stay the night like he promised. He told me that he couldn't, but that he would return the next day as he was going to bring me the bottle of the pain pills he had requested for me. Frankly, I was more concerned that he was leaving than about the pills.

I said, "Please stay Hijo (Spanish for "son"), stay." At that moment, we were at the front door of our house, and he was holding his beautiful Yorkshire Terrier, Bella. He said, "I have to go, mom, I have to go. I have to take care of a few things." He softly kissed my cheek and left. That was the last time I saw my son alive.

As the day turned into night, I drifted in and out of sleep. The following day was Tuesday, and strangely I did not hear from Jorge. Around 2:00 p.m. , I asked my husband if he had heard from Jorge. He said, yes, that Jorge had told him that he would be coming over. But we didn't hear from him the rest of the day. My husband, George, found out that Jorge had picked up the Hydrocodone prescription. He was quite troubled by that news. But when he spoke with Jorge, my son told him that he was coming over later that afternoon with the medication. I didn't feel very good that day, so I did not attempt to call him or text him. We both believed he was coming over later that day.

Wednesday arrived, and I still felt very sick and was in a great deal of pain. The morning went by quickly as I slept and took my pain medication as prescribed. My husband was in and out of the house, taking care of some important matters as I rested. Around 3:30 p.m. I awoke to the ringing of my cell phone and as I looked, it was Jorge. I answered only to discover that he was in great anguish. He was speaking fast and telling me so many things at the same time that it confused and overwhelmed me.

I had no idea what was going on as he began to complain incessantly. I became quite upset and begged him to stop. I asked him, "What's going on Hijo? I said, you must take control of your problems because you are out of control. You have been overwhelming me with great distress since the day before my surgery and you have made this all about you. You have created nothing but chaos at a time when I need to rest and be at peace so I can heal properly." He then yelled at me saying, "I'm 'really' going to kill myself now!" With that, he hung up on me.

Soon after that he sent me a text that read, "Delete my number from your phone and George's phone. Don't contact me again. Forget about me!" Immediately I called my mom who was like another mother for my son; she had helped me raise him since I was living with my parents when he was born. My mother heard my agony, confusion, and pain. She advised me to turn my cell phone off. She said that I needed to take care of myself, and at this rate, Jorge was going to drive me insane. She said that it was very selfish of him to be causing me such trouble in my condition. She advised me not to call him, which I didn't.

Now, when I look back on that day, I see more clearly what was going on. He had been abusing Hydrocodone for nine months and suddenly stopped taking it just two weeks before. I grieve to this day for failing to understand the consequences of suddenly stopping Hydrocodone or other painkillers after taking higher doses than prescribed without proper supervision and treatment.

Late that night, I drifted in and out of sleep, still heavily medicated due to the pain. I remember seeing the time on my clock—**11:57 p.m.** I was awake, in a foggy state, half asleep for the next two hours. I seemed to hear voices next to me repeating in unison, "Nothing is impossible for God. Nothing is impossible for God. Nothing is impossible for God." Finally, I fell asleep sometime after 2:00 a.m.

The following day was uneventful. I rested, trusting that everything would be okay. My husband did not speak with Jorge that day as he was focused on caring for me. All I did that day was sleep, trying to recover.

As Friday morning arrived, I sent a text message to my son, asking if he was going to come over and stay for at least a few days through the weekend. I was still uneasy because I hadn't heard from him in a couple of days. The hours passed, and I did not hear back from him at all that day.

I had no idea that I would be facing the absolute worst moment of my life in just a few short hours. An emotional earthquake was going to strike with such ferocity that nothing in me could stand. This earthquake would not involve losing material possessions as I endured before in my native country Nicaragua. It wasn't about losing social and economic status, friends, culture or my home country. No, this earthquake would bring devastation unlike any I had previously experienced.

Around 3:30 p.m. that afternoon, Jorge's best friend, called me to ask if I had heard from Jorge. I told him that Jorge got upset with me on Wednesday afternoon and that I hadn't heard from him since. I tried to assure him that Jorge was probably okay. He was just having one of his typical fits when we disagree. But his friend was concerned that nobody had heard from him for two days, which was quite unusual for a social butterfly like Jorge. He said that everybody had been trying to reach him, but were unable to get any response. He said he was afraid something bad had happened. He asked me if someone had gone to Jorge's house. I said, "No, I am in bed, and George is taking care of me." He told me that he had a job interview that afternoon, but he was going to cancel it and go to Jorge's house to check on him. I didn't say anything to anyone, but I was fearful.

Terror Has Come

One hour later, my phone rang. This time the ring felt inexplicably different. When I answered, I was gripped with fear as I heard Jorge's friend yell, *"He's gone! He's gone! Jorge is gone! He went to Heaven!"*

I couldn't understand anything else he said, between his crying, sobbing and talking. But I did hear him say, "He's gone! Jorge is gone!" There it was, the earthquake with devastation unlike I had ever known. I had been through physical earthquakes, but nothing could prepare me for this. I couldn't think. I simply couldn't process what I was hearing. I didn't want to hear what he was saying to me.

I walked as fast I could to my husband's office in our house. He was there alone. I was trembling so hard, shaking to my core. I handed the phone to him and said "It's Jorge's friend (Name Omitted)." I stood there and watched my husband's face suddenly grow pale. He began to shake his head in shock. "What, are you sure?" he stuttered.

Filled with every imaginable emotion, I can remember crossing the street, going to my friend's house. I didn't even think to put anything on my feet. I remember a gentle breeze softly hitting my face. For a split-second, I felt an unexpected peace in my heart. I sensed that my life moving forward would be forever changed. That moment was very surreal; one I will never forget. I rang and rang my neighbor's doorbell relentlessly.

When she opened the door, she said, "Are you okay Jessica? Are you in pain? Where is George? You have no shoes. Where is George? Jessica, what's going on?"

I somehow I managed to blurt out "My Jorge is dead!" She responded, "Oh Jessica, no! Where is George? Let's go to your house." Coming to the realization of what I had just said, I lost my ability to speak for the next three days.

She walked me back home, holding my hand. As we made our way to the front door of the house, George came and met us. His face was indescribably different. My friend asked him, "George, what happened to Jorge?" At that moment, I instinctively hid behind her trying to protect myself from what I knew in my heart. I did not want to hear the words come out of his mouth as I knew they would be true.

George whispered to her, "He's dead!" Then she asked him, "Are you sure? Is it true?" George nodded his head. "Yes," he said softly.

I barely remember the events of the next several days, except for a few small snapshots inside my head. I remember everyone making sure I stayed on my medication. They wanted to help me avoid serious complications from the surgery just one week earlier. They were also concerned I might experience a nervous breakdown or even a heart attack, because of the overwhelming emotional and physical pain I was experiencing having lost my dear child.

At some point, I picked up my cell phone and opened my messages. I realized I had received a text from my son on Wednesday at **11:57 p.m.** that read—"Get Bella." I began to sob uncontrollably as I called out for Bella, the 11-month-old Yorkie that Jorge adored. All I could do was hold Bella in my arms and cry. Jorge had entrusted me with his most precious and only true possession. His text to me was to say, "I trust you Mom," which I knew in my heart was his way of saying, "Goodbye."

My mother and my sister-in-law took the first flight they could catch out of Central America. They arrived in Houston on Sunday, March 13, 2011. Mom couldn't wait to be with me. I wasn't the only one losing a son; she was as well. Finally Jorge's "two moms" could mourn his death together.

My Son Killed Himself

Chapter Two
THE EARLY YEARS

To recall and write about these events is very emotionally difficult for me. I remember how amazing the period was when I lived in my parents' house. Immediately it brings a smile to my face and happiness to my heart. Sometimes when I remember those days and realize that they are gone forever, it somehow stirs a sense of deep emotional conflict within my soul.

It's never easy when the trials and tribulations of life take you through the fire. Yet through the trials and in the fire I am able to more clearly understand the Scripture—

> "And we know that all things work together for good to those who love God, to those who are the called according to *His* purpose" (Romans 8:28 NKJV).

Those early years brought no indication of our suffering and sadness that was to come. Our home, especially with Jorge with us, was a small slice of Heaven on earth. They were truly the best days of my son's life and ours as a family. The word "family" is easy to pronounce, but sometimes difficult to maintain.

My objective in writing this chapter and sharing these events is to emphasize how important it is that children are raised and nurtured in a loving God-centered home. My goal is to raise awareness of this vital area of our children's lives.

I have met so many people who carry deep emotional wounds, scars, severe pain and a dysfunctional sense of self. As my relationship with the Father God has grown deeper over the last 12 years, I have seen this with greater insight and clarity than any other time in my life. Many of the people I have met and talked to have been deeply wounded as children. It's shocking to see how much emotional damage comes to a child or teen as a direct result of a lack of love and unity in the family.

Our amazing God sees the family as something else. It's a place of belonging, unconditional love, structure, service, safety and security. Sadly, many in our society have strayed far from this godly, loving plan and are reaping tragedy as the unintended consequence.

My Early Life

I adored being with my family. I was born in Managua, Nicaragua into a family with a high social status. Our family name was widely recognized, and we were blessed with a good life. But above all, the most important and essential part of our family was love. Love is such a small word to convey the feeling and emotion embodied within it. Sometimes the English language fails to describe what is truly in my heart.

When I was 17 years old, I married Jorge's father, also named Jorge. Because of the massive chaos our country was experiencing, many people were marrying very young. The first year we lived in my grandmother Mami's house. Later we moved to my mother's house; and afterward to a neighbor's house who had fled Nicaragua for about six months. After being married for two years, our bliss faded quickly as my husband's ideas of marriage and family didn't agree with mine. We were two irresponsible teenagers, which did not help. Marriage is for adults. Shortly after that, I discovered I was pregnant. Meanwhile, my husband and I were separating. Our marriage had no potential because of his extreme irresponsibility.

Getting married so young, how could I have known that I had married into a family with a long lineage of alcoholism, emotional dysfunction, etc. It is incredible to me how blinded we can become when choosing our spouses. Science would have us believe that a percentage of addiction is not only a predisposition but also inherited. No matter the "findings" of science or what science says, as adults we are individually responsible to choose whether to act upon those predisposed genetic tendencies and desires. If not then we are nothing more than robots operating at the whim of whatever desires our bodies, will, mind and emotions dictate. One certainly exists and that is we are born with a 100% sin nature, and we have 100% choice of whether we are going to act upon those desires.

After Jorge's father had left to live in the United States (Miami, Florida) with his parents, I moved back into my parents' home in Nicaragua, as is typical in my culture. At age

19, I was still considered just a "child" for in the Latin culture a person isn't considered to have reached full maturity until the age of 25 years old. It was such a blessing to know that my parents' home was always open no matter what mistakes I'd made and a symbol of my parent's unconditional love for and commitment to me. My mom, dad and Mami were an incredible support system, always there to love and protect me.

The Nicaraguan civil revolution brought incredible turmoil, difficulty and uncertainty to our lives unlike we had ever known. I was "mostly" distressed by the loss of my marriage (divorce) was not traditionally accepted in Latin-American culture, which is still the same today. We support the family unit and marriage of husband and wife/mother and father at all costs.

Soon, the tragedy of being divorced, losing sight of everything I had known plus the fact that I was pregnant was overwhelming. Then suddenly I found myself with the necessity to move to a new country with barely anything but my name and my baby growing inside of me. It was hard to describe what was happening to us and how it affected us.

While in the last trimester of my pregnancy with Jorge, my home country of Nicaragua was going through a massive revolution. The Sandinistas had won the revolution in July of 1979, now five years later, this totalitarian regime, was facing a contra-revolution. Our family did their best to withstand as long as we could. Ultimately, we had to make the heart-wrenching decision to leave our native land.

Nicaraguans were suffering under the oppressive, revolutionary communist regime that indoctrinated the people by permeating the radio, television and education systems. An overwhelming amount of social hatred raged against the church. Massive numbers of people in support of the communist regime were in the streets carrying chains, wooden clubs, and all sorts of objects to cause pain and destruction to private property.

The government finally crossed the line for our family when it became likely that my brother would have to enlist in an unjust civil war. My parents were finally prepared to escape to Honduras with our family. My grandmother was a powerful woman who adored us and watched over us for many years. From the day I was born, I was the "apple" of my Mami's eye. She helped us escape Nicaragua after the Sandinistas gained complete control, and the country under communist control.

New Place, New Time

Our lives changed dramatically in every worldly sense after we fled. We had little money and a name that didn't hold any clout in our new country. We had no extended family there. We were no longer held in high esteem. Suddenly we had no friends, and we had nothing we could count on but each other. The only thing that we could depend on was the most amazing thing of all; it was the glue that held us together. We had love. It was into this environment my son Jorge was born.

Jorge was saturated his first eight years with the love of my entire family—myself, my parents, and, of course, my beloved grandmother, Mami. In no time, little Jorge became my grandma's entire world. He was her reason to live and the center of her life. I was so young I had no idea what being a mother entailed. I relied heavily on my parents and Mami for guidance. Jorge secured and surrounded in a "cocoon of love." My grandmother, my mother, and my father adored him. As the years went by, I felt more like Jorge's sister than his mother. After losing all that we had in Nicaragua, he was the one precious gift that I retained. He was my world, and I was annoyed that I had to share him with so many people. I dreamed of a day when I would be Jorge's one and only mother and be able to make all the decisions for us both. I often fantasized about building a life with a husband and Jorge.

Latin culture is overprotective, and hierarchy is primary making it very difficult for me to clearly establish my role as a mother. I was third in line as far as Jorge was concerned. My grandmother was first, then my mother, and then me. I was perceived as too immature to make viable decisions for my son and myself. In the daily decisions concerning Jorge, my opinions or desires were often disregarded. I soon realized I wasn't mature enough, and in time, I lost my sense of identity.

Jorge, the one precious gift I had been given was treated differently than my brother, and I. The structure and boundaries that applied to us did not apply to my "little bundle of joy." He was always the exception to the rule.

Having left Nicaragua, our lives changed radically. Mami turned all her love, power and attention over to my son Jorge. Due to her position in the family and the respect she deserved, it was difficult to oppose her. She maintained her financial independence even more so, which was a big problem. Not only was Jorge given everything he wanted without regard for the rest of the household, but it was also impossible to reprimand him. If he did something that mother or I considered inappropriate, it was virtually impossible for me to correct him due to my grandma's interference.

Our house was always a place where you felt safe and loved. A place where the world couldn't penetrate and hurt you. Even if you were in pain somehow, you could still find protection and healing. It was a place where one would want to spend the rest of their life.

It was not always perfect. We had financial issues, disagreements, illnesses, and other typical challenges. My brother and I got into trouble as teenagers often do. We were by all accounts a normal family. Many times I confronted my mother's belief system calling her "antiquated." I thank the Lord for her firm stand and that she never compromised. What set our home apart was the love we practiced within our family, and the foundation and source of this love.

My parents held firm to their Catholic Christian values that outlined the parameters in which we lived. The values were all encompassing. It began with unconditional love, but also encompassed selflessness, giving, forgiveness, and kindness. I clearly remember how when my brother and I would fight, my dad would sit us down on the sofa and command us to apologize to each other. We had to make peace by kissing each other on the cheek before either of us moved from the couch. We were taught to be considerate and thoughtful to one another, to have mercy, and to offer second chances. Boundaries were established to protect us in every possible area.

My parents were vigilant about the people with whom we associated and quickly recognized destructive habits. Rules were established to protect us and help us thrive. In our home, everyone knew they belonged. Respect was given and received; we understood forgiveness, and we were accepted. Our home was a place of refuge, healing, restoration, provision and safety. We were our parent's most precious possessions. Nothing could separate us from my family's love and protection. For many reasons our home consistently had an atmosphere of joy, no matter what problems we had.

We began to understand the beauty, simplicity and peace of the unfailing, unconditional love that God alone gives. As devoted Catholics, we were taught to serve God by serving others, to fear Him and have reverence toward Him. Our home was a place where God had the prominent position of authority. We taught how to exercise faith and our parents led by example. We learned to surrender everything to the Lord.

His commandments and teachings became so rooted in my life as clearly commanded in the Book of Proverbs—

"Train up a child in the way he should go, and when he is old, he will not depart from it" (Proverbs 22:6 NKJV).

I have come to realize how true those words are. I pray that you come to this understanding as you continue to read. Consequently, this type of family life made it easier for me to understand God's heart towards us, His unconditional love for us, His guidance, as well as His discipline. The Bible refers to love as the greatest of all commandments—to love the Lord your God with all your heart and to love one another (Matthew 22:37). Parents in a Catholic Latin home teach their children Scriptures concerning love and family from their birth.

Love

"Though I speak with the tongues of men and of angels but have not love, I have become sounding brass or a clanging cymbal. And though I have the gift of prophecy, and understand all mysteries and all knowledge, and though I have all faith, so that I could remove mountains, but have not love, I am nothing. And though I bestow all my goods to feed the poor, and though I give my body to be burned but have not love, it profits me nothing. Love suffers long and is kind; love does not envy; love does not parade itself, is not puffed up; does not behave rudely, does not seek its own, is not provoked, thinks no evil; does not rejoice in iniquity, but rejoices in the truth; bears all things, believes all things, hopes all things, endures all things. Love never fails. And now these three remain: faith, hope and love. But the greatest of these is love" (1 Corinthians 13:1-8, 13 NKJV).

One of my mother's favorite Scripture verses was from 1 Corinthians which talks about love and the attributes of love. Growing up I learned that true love is more than just a word because it is a word that requires action. Love involves two different concepts:

— The first concept is endearing affection or absolute obligation with minimal feeling behind it. My parents knew this very well. If we aren't careful, duties of love can easily become obligations. My heart is burdened seeing so many children today who only feel their parents' obligatory love every day. Some parents even try to free themselves from the trouble, the responsibility placed upon them as a result of their having children. Children sense the emptiness in the words "I love you" when the words are spoken out of obligation.

They don't understand that love is not simply an emotional whim that comes and goes like the ebb and flow of the tide that embraces the shoreline. Love is a willful, purposeful and intentional. My parents' love was established on an unshakeable foundation of commitment and responsibility. Commitment is the basic footing upon which love is rooted and established. Responsibility requires doing what is right. It also means not acting on a whim or out of a selfish desire, which has become commonplace in today's society.

— The second concept is that genuine love requires total loyalty, reliability, unity, and faithfulness. Love is impossible without a sacrifice. Love is a balance of giving and placing others' needs and desires before our own. Love gives respect freely because authentic love holds the loved one in high esteem. A spirit of joy is crucial for a happy family, and in my parents' home joy was present no matter what circumstances we faced.

Joy isn't an emotion, unlike happiness. It doesn't come and go. Joy remains where love is. Joy is a by-product of the Holy Spirit at work within us producing the fruit of joy. Love is justice because it does not act on self-interest. Love contains boundaries, discipline and at times, punishment. Love doesn't make you an enabler for bad, destructive or irresponsible behaviors. Sound love will also correct, rebuke, chastise, teach, guide, train and exhort.

The origin of man and his final destiny are permeated with God's perfect love in a collection of 66 Books called the Bible. The Bible is the open display of God's plan and purpose for man—"All Scripture is given by inspiration of God, and is profitable for doctrine, for reproof, for correction, for instruction in righteousness, that the man of God may be complete, thoroughly equipped for every good work" (2 Timothy 3:16-17 NKJV).

Simply put, pure love is manifest and on display in all of its glory in the attributes of Jesus Christ Himself. We can begin to understand the fullness of love as we understand God the Father more, and observe the various facets of his character. The fundamental principal of God's love is truth and mercy and commitment.

God is love! He is the ultimate and complete example of true love. He never fails us. He teaches us to love in a proper and balanced way; to never elevate our personal worth in vain conceit, nor to diminish ourselves by self-condemnation. The love of God is steady, solid, unshakeable and impenetrable. It is this type of love that He deposits into His children to bear for one another. In the community, love is based upon social grace, treating one another as we want to be treated. Within the church (brothers and sisters in Christ) it is an endearing love. Finally, the family structure should embody a love that encompasses all the attributes of God; justly established and demonstrated in and through His Word, the Bible. Love aside from this foundation is false; it is a mirage and is dangerous.

Even though my son Jorge grew up in a loving family structure, that structure had been fractured due to our having left our homeland. Family love still functioned, but discipline was defiled. Jorge and I felt sheltered and protected until a series of events reframed our circumstances, and we took a sharp turn for the worse.

As I write these words, my intense prayer for you is that the Lord will equip and enlighten you to understand that God-based love is vital for the emotional well-being of our children. Raising our children in an environment of divine love is necessary for them to be emotionally whole, complete with nothing missing.

This type of love will save them from all forms of destruction. We parents and caregivers should fight to maintain this loving ambiance in our homes for our children. Their lives and futures are worthy of the sacrifice. The divine love that God shows us each day is the same type of love that God desires for our families.

God desires His love for our families yet in today's society selfishness has taken root, defiling this type of love. Everywhere you will see children roaming our streets without boundaries or structures trying to make sense of their spoiled lives. Many have developed a spirit of entitlement, arrogance, and rebellion. Some trying desperately to escape the sorrow and pain of a dysfunctional family, often fleeing a center of rejection, rather than one of love. Many times to gain the love and attention they desire, they start associating with the wrong crowd. Soon they begin abusing various illegal drugs, prescription drugs, and alcohol, some to the point of suicide. Many times because we have not surrendered to God, submitting our minds, hearts, will and emotions to His wisdom.

The Word of the Lord is clear about the way we should behave in our marriages, families, and toward one another in the body of Christ. I am very aware that the secular world mocks and ridicules these verses. Before I go on, it is imperative for me to share the following Scriptures that not only show appreciative and honorable behavior, but they also create a picture of the correct structure in the family household. They illustrate the foundation of Christ as the Head and exalt the union of husband and wife—

> "Therefore, as the elect of God, holy and beloved, put on tender mercies, kindness, humility, meekness, longsuffering; bearing with one another, and forgiving one another, if

anyone has a complaint against another; even as Christ forgave you, so you also must do. But above all these things put on love, which is the bond of perfection. And let the peace of God rule in your hearts, to which also you were called in one body; and be thankful. Let the word of Christ dwell in you richly in all wisdom, teaching and admonishing one another in psalms and hymns and spiritual songs, singing with grace in your hearts to the Lord. And whatever you do in word or deed, do all in the name of the Lord Jesus, giving thanks to God the Father through Him" (Colossians 3: 12-17 NKJV).

"Wives, submit to your own husbands, as is fitting in the Lord. Husbands love your wives and do not be bitter toward them. Children, obey your parents in all things, for this is well-pleasing to the Lord. Fathers, do not provoke your children, lest they become discouraged" (Colossians 3: 18-21 NKJV).

"Husbands, likewise, dwell with them with understanding, giving honor to the wife, as to the weaker vessel, and as being heirs together of the grace of life, that your prayers may not be hindered" (1 Peter 3:7 NKJV).

Chapter Three
SEEKING A FATHER

"...Jesus cried with a loud voice, Eli, Eli, lama sabachthani?—that is, My God, My God, why have You abandoned Me [leaving Me helpless, forsaking and failing Me in My need]" (Matthew 27:46 AMP)?

The last words which were spoken by Jesus on the cross before His death were during a terrible hour—even for the King of Kings and Lord of Lords. He who intimately knew the Father and was one with Him embodied the sin of all mankind and became sin on our behalf as His Father turned His face from Him. God is Holy and in Him there is no darkness. He cannot look upon sin without passing judgment. Jesus' darkest hour was when the Father abandoned Him for a moment. What a desperate cry as Jesus realized He was separated from God, His Father!

I would like to discuss a topic that lately has affected our society in a very detrimental way. Society today suffers from an identity crisis. Let's talk about Identity. The word Identity comes from the Latin word *Identitās*, which means sameness or oneness. One of the definitions of the word Identity is the set of behavioral or personal characteristics by which an individual is recognizable as a member of a group (family, culture, and group).

In one of my visits to a noted Psychotherapist Dr. Red* (name changed), he explained to me in detail how identity develops within the nest of a family:

> "In a family, a father identifies with his wife and a wife identifies with her husband. Meaning that they each honor and respect both the person and the positions they each hold; and that they are willing to be transparent to one another in all issues about this covenant. Their combined identities form the basis of all family values for themselves and their children who identify with them."

Let me break this down for you starting with an example when my son Jorge was only seven years old. One day I opened the door to the room where my grandmother, Jorge, and I used to sleep. As I opened the door, I saw Jorge dressed in my grandma's clothing, including her special orthopedic shoes. He was viewing himself in the mirror and talking to himself as my grandmother would.

I mentioned to you before how we had fled our native country Nicaragua and how it impacted our lives. We were living in Honduras, but as I mentioned before, due to tradition within the Latin culture my grandmother held the highest position of authority and respect. Contrary to what most people believe, Latin culture is more matriarchal than patriarchal. At least this was how my family functioned.

I ran to speak with my mother about what I'd seen Jorge doing, assuming that she, a wise woman, would know what to do. She told me that we were going to make an appointment with the best child psychologist in the capital city. You might be thinking why I was so alarmed, children often do this type of stuff? I was alarmed because Mami and Jorge had a very special bond as if they were one. This was very alarming to me. It was clear to me how deeply Jorge was being affected by her dysfunctional, extremely-overprotective love. They had identified so completely with each other that it was difficult to see where one ended, and the other began.

As I was saying, we took Jorge in for an evaluation that lasted three or four days. His evaluation involved several types of tests. Each day he spent no less than three hours at the doctor's office with a group of specialists in child development and behavior. After Jorge had spent multiple days interacting with the specialists, many diagnosis and conclusions were drawn. Finally, the primary specialist of the group explained the findings to both me and my mother, and he explained everything broken into two main categories— *Intelligence Quotient (IQ)* and *Family Structure*:

— First, they determined that Jorge had an extremely high *IQ*. The primary specialist told my mother and me that it would likely be difficult for us to raise him. He congratulated me for being so young and told me that I was going to need a lot of energy to care for him. Also, he said that in contrast to what many people believe, most individuals with high IQ levels are unsuccessful in society. There are many reasons for this, however, the primary being that they typically learn to rely on their "own" talents and abilities that enable them get away with virtually anything. On top of that, Jorge had a lethal combination of charm, well-developed social skills and grace, a cute face and charismatic personality.

The doctor told us that children with normal IQ levels learned to depend on efforts and hard work to achieve their goals, learning little by little self-control and self-discipline. He said this is why most normal IQ people became successful, unlike the high IQ persons who learn to rely on their innate skills, talents, visions and ideas. These factors clearly demonstrated that we would have a challenging and difficult task ahead. Looking back on this brings so much pain because, in my ignorance, I lost my son.

— Second, the doctor addressed the *Family Structure*. He explained how children will imitate the most dominant person in the household. He said children are not stupid, and they don't want to appear weak. Consequently, they will identify with the person with the most dominant characteristics within the family structure. In this case, Jorge identified with his grandmother due to the control she exercised in the household. He recommended family therapy to put the roles of each person within the family back in proper order for Jorge's benefit. Sadly, this wasn't possible due to the authority my grandmother had over our household. She thought all this was pure baloney.

Looking back, I feel a deep sense of guilt as I remember reading romance novels instead of taking the time to learn how to be a mother. I doubt that I could have exercised much power within our family structure. I would have most likely been ignored, disregarded and overlooked but maybe this is just a cheap excuse and an attempt to comfort myself.

Getting back to Dr. Red's comments, I will do my best to explain what he shared about a person's identity and how it is shaped—

The mother plays an important and crucial role for the emotional benefit of the child. Likewise, the father plays a specific and equally critical role in the family. Each is to respect and honor the other's distinct position in the household. Each aligns their behavior within those roles, learning how to manage specific tasks and responsibilities while supporting the other. In this mutually respectful environment, children find not only emotional security and well-being but also find common ground with, learn respect and honor for the position each parent, identifying with them both.

The father is to provide a stable source of strength and sound mind. He is the guard, the faithful protector of the household; not only because of his physical and natural strength but for his innate ability to judge things dispassionately. He provides the comfort of security. His high sense of commitment and integrity make him the focus of the family's honor. At the same time, his natural physical strength can play a big part when demanding respect and exercising authority. Each member of the household is accountable to him for their behavior. Even the deep tone of his voice supports that.

In contrast, the mother is to nurture the family with comfort, love, and unconditional care. She is the best person to have next to you during times of sickness, sorrow, and happiness. She tends to be emotional by nature. She can be sensitive, sweet and noble-hearted. She is committed to her husband and her children. Because she is strong at heart, her commitment goes beyond all of life's challenges.

The roles of both spouses fit together like a hand in glove. They are perfectly and strategically designed to develop and nurture children, and to help them learn the basic foundations of the social structure. As a result, both husband and wife (father and mother, male and female) represent a perfect balance creating an opportunity for the God ordained outcome.

As the children begin to identify the positions, authorities and roles each parent plays, they begin to develop their individual gender identification accordingly. As a son matures, the mother starts to distance herself from him to enable the father to nurture the boy and allow him to absorb his skills and mannerisms. Similarly, the girl starts to imagine the role she will have as she begins to see herself as a mother.

It is sad to see how far society has drifted from the original, perfect and well-organized structure of the family foundation. The original design offers the best outcome for our society. When God felt that it wasn't good for man to be alone, He created Eve, Adam's perfect mate and perfect fit, from one of Adam's ribs. After God had formed the woman, He commanded them to multiply. This union is so sacred that God demanded—

"For this reason a man should leave his father and mother and be united to his wife, and they will become one flesh" (Genesis 2:24 NKJV).

When this union is altered, disrupted, destroyed, broken or falsely imitated, it brings an imbalance within the family unit that adversely affects each member, potentially developing dysfunction that will affect our entire society. Proper balance in family structure is imperative to operate one's family, according to God's plan. When that is not possible, as in the case of a broken home, a single parent should seek shelter, a sense of community, and advice from the church that is the family of God. In this way, even a broken family will continue to operate under Godly principles of love and structure for the benefit of each member.

Jorge grew up without a father in his life causing many internal struggles though we were unaware of this problem. We had no idea how dramatically this would impact his future. My mom was always worried about it, but we simply did not understand the dire consequences this would bring to his life.

In those years, divorce in the Latin culture wasn't socially acceptable or common. Consequently, we didn't observe many examples of the catastrophic damage a lack of a father figure would cause to someone's identity. We are heartbroken by the fact that we didn't understand how Jorge felt. We only knew that he didn't have a father like his friends did. The only father figure he could relate to was my father, who as the only male in the house was typically outnumbered and overruled by the women in the house. Being a peaceful and quiet gentleman, he took the back seat and allowed the women to run the show. Consequently, a lack of balance within the family structure was created which also had similar impacts within Jorge.

I have learned that when something as small as a single hair is outside God's ordained family structure, literally the gates of hell will seize the opportunity. It may not be visible at the moment, but at some point it will appear, in the individual, family, or both. Barring a miracle of God, one or both will eventually become dysfunctional. I understand these are unsavory words that no one wants to hear, but it's true whether we like it or not.

A noted sociologist who has done extensive research in the field of fathers and fatherhood observed that fathers bring tremendous benefits into the home, unlike any other are able to bring. The connection between father and child will directly impact the child's cognitive ability, educational achievement, psychological well-being, and even social behavior.

Jorge was about five and one-half years old when he first met his father. His grandfather was coming to Nicaragua and called us ahead of time to ask if we could meet him in Nicaragua because he wanted to see Jorge, his grandchild. Knowing how important this was in my culture, my mother and I arranged to go from Honduras to Nicaragua and meet him. When we arrived, he begged us to allow him to take Jorge to meet his father in Miami, Florida. At this time, Jorge spoke perfectly and was unusually smart. My mom and I discussed this at length. Knowing the importance of Jorge knowing his biological father, we allowed him to go.

After he had returned from Miami, the first thing that Jorge said was that his dad didn't love him. When we asked him what he meant by that, he told us that his dad didn't care what type of food or candy he ate. He said that his dad didn't make sure he bathed or brushed his teeth before going to bed. Little Jorge interpreted that to mean that his father didn't love him. One day out of nowhere he said, "Don't make me go to visit my dad again, he doesn't care for me or love me." After that incident, he didn't mention his dad again until he was a young teenager.

Shortly after this event a relative from my mother's side of the family came to live in Honduras. He became very close to Jorge, and since Jorge was growing up without a dominant role model in his life, we allowed them to get close. Soon, the man became Jorge's hero. He held a prominent place in Jorge's life from the time he was six until he was 12 years old.

After a few years, I was convinced Jorge was in good hands. So, I married an American and left Honduras for the United States with the promise Jorge would be joining us soon.

The United States

As I recall these years my heart is filled with sadness. I know there were hidden secrets to Jorge's brokenness and the destruction of his male identity. He never really connected and formulated his male gender identity during the most critical years of his development.

I came to the United States with such great anticipation of building a life for me and Jorge. My heart was filled with dreams and desires to create a family and an opportunity that when Jorge joined me he would finally find the father figure he so desperately craved. Sadly the life I found when I arrived was nothing like I anticipated and when Jorge joined me the dreams I had for the two of us quickly turned into a nightmare. Jorge didn't find the father figure he craved, and I couldn't create the family I hoped to find. The lone bright spot in the midst of this nightmare was that I became pregnant with my youngest son, a mere five months after my arrival.

Once I left Nicaragua, I was issued a Visa and granted residency in Honduras. When I received U.S. residency, my residency in Honduras was immediately terminated since it wasn't my homeland. Suddenly, I had no country to which I could return, even if I wanted to.

Even though Jorge was a Honduran citizen, I could not establish legal residency in Honduras again. That left me with no way out. I didn't know the English language and had no idea of what sort of work I could do. I had never worked before. I held a temporary residency for two years. Certainly this was not the life I envisioned. I was trapped in a nightmare. I couldn't go anywhere. It was never my intention to move to the United States or to marry an American to "have rights." My only plan was for Jorge and me to have a family, our own home, and a place where we were loved, protected, accepted and respected. Sadly this was not our life upon arriving in the United States.

As I mentioned before, in Nicaragua and Honduras I enjoyed the most established and nearly perfect family structure for the first twenty years of my life. My father adored my mother. I never once heard him yell at her nor witness any disrespect. When Jorge came to live with me, he was excited, hoping to find a father and a father figure. Instead, he found himself sent back and forth between America and Honduras repeatedly over the next five years. He never finished a SINGLE school year in one country.

My mom and grandmother begged me to allow Jorge to come back and live with them because of the unhealthy environment. So I had no choice but to allow him to go back to Honduras for his good, but he cried for me, and I cried for him. My husband at the time promised me things were going to be okay, that we just needed a little more time. I brought Jorge back to the United States, again and again. Each time he would arrive, he would cry for his "mothers" in Honduras saying he missed them. He continued to search for his father figure here but each time as he continued to find rejection, I would allow him to go back again.

While all this was happening, the man who had become Jorge's hero in Honduras, whom he loved, trusted and admired, did the unthinkable to him. To punish Jorge for "disobeying" him, he pulled down Jorge's pants and poured acid over his genitals. This event profoundly damaged him. I feel such profound sadness. Many times I think to myself and wonder what could I have done differently. If only I could go back in time and change something, but I can't. These events were instrumental in Jorge's life and a foundation for his destruction and a blatant attack on his identity!

Finally FREE in the United States

After six and a half years, I got divorced. Jorge returned once again at 13 years of age and this time, he had arrived for good. Finally, he was with me and his five-year-old brother. We were going to start our life together as a family. I determined that my children were going to have to depend on me since I could not find the Godly and honorable man like my daddy was.

Reflecting for a bit here, I see that the main problem wasn't only that I was a single parent. The real problem was that I was at best, a worldly Christian, or what some would call a secular-Christian. Despite my having been raised in a practicing Catholic home and a parochial school, I didn't follow the laws of God closely. Sometimes I think, if I had "really" known God during this time of my life, so many devastating issues would have been avoided. I hope you and others will learn from my pain, confusion, and rebellion.

Keep Going

Those first six and a half years were extremely hard years, and we endured difficult trials after arriving in the United States, but we were happy because we were together. The trials continued, but we were able to keep going and every trial that came our way we overcame them all, as a family.

From Bad to Worse

One day Jorge really managed to surprise me. For anyone that ever knew Jorge would understand that he was full of surprises. It was around Thanksgiving, one day I arrived home from work to find that somehow, Jorge had traveled to Miami, Florida on his own to meet his dad. In my panic, I discovered that his father's aunt had sent him an airline ticket so he could get acquainted with his dad and his extended family. I knew very little about his dad's family, so I was franticly trying to go after him.

As a single mother of two, in my despair I was trying to figure out every conceivable way to make my way to Miami. I quickly found a way and boarded a plane to Florida. After arriving safely at Jorge's aunt's house and once I worked my way through a wide range of emotions, she convinced me to allow him to stay with them for a while. She told me it was important that I get established in my new life, and she stressed how important it was for Jorge to get to know them. I agreed because Jorge wanted to do this, and I also believed it would be good for Jorge to get to know some of his family in the United States. I realized, after seeing his brother with a father who adored him and was beyond crazy for him, Jorge also needed to find his own father. So with tears in my eyes I boarded a plane back to Houston.

Once again Jorge's life was about to take a dramatic turn for the worse. With great expectation, Jorge showed up to meet his father for the first time since he was five years old. He stood at the front door of his father's house ringing the doorbell, needing the acceptance of a father who has rejected him for his entire life. Standing on the front porch wondering if he will be accepted or rejected. Then his father answers the door and speaks words of rejection that will split his heart in two. Words of rejection that will wound him for the rest of his life. For Jorge as a teenager the ultimate words or rejection when his father told him, "I don't love you, I don't ever want to see you again, leave and never come back." He received no sense of approval or validation from his father. I cannot tell you how profoundly this damaged and hurt Jorge. His natural father rejected him again, but this time in the most dramatic and tragic way. You can't begin to imagine how devastating this was for Jorge at an age when he desperately needed his father.

As I told you, I knew very little about his dad's family, but they called me to let me know what had happened with Jorge's dad. They reassured me that Jorge's dad wasn't the only person in that family who loved Jorge. His grandparents wanted to give Jorge a chance to establish a relationship with his dad's side of the family.

I was prepared to get on the first plane back to Miami but I spoke with Jorge, and he told me that he wanted to stay. Although I felt uneasy about it, I finally agreed, not knowing why until later. I discovered that his aunt had a female cousin who had lived with her for the past sixteen years as her lesbian lover. As Jorge settled in, they decided to take him shopping at the most expensive Italian fashion designers' stores in Miami. They also took him to Europe showing him the best the world had to offer. They wanted a son and a family which they couldn't naturally produce.

When Jorge turned 15 years, the housekeeper who worked for his aunt called to tell me that Jorge's aunts had introduced him to a friend of theirs who was gay so that Jorge could start dating. They had made the determination that Jorge was gay, and he needed to embrace and accept his identity. I had gone to see Jorge twice, hoping to bring him home with me. Both times he refused. Deception blinded him. He was promised money, and all that money could buy. Finally, I was able to find a way to rescue Jorge from this toxic and inappropriate environment, but it already had lethal consequences for his soul. The battle I had after he came back home was huge, but after a little time he had seemed to have returned to normal, but it was only in appearance.

Jorge continued with high school and started working. Things seemed to be okay, but one too many drops of water filled the glass causing it to overflow. Jorge's great-grandmother in Honduras, Mami, one of the main pillars in his life, died. She was the one who was always there, unmovable, unconditionally loving and accepting him. She was the love of his life. In one sense, to him, she was "his real mother." He went to Honduras a few days before me for the funeral, and I followed him as she was also my love, my Mami.

I recall at the last minute when the casket was about to be placed in the mausoleum, Jorge stopped the men and asked them to open the casket. The entire family was there, yet we all allowed it because we knew how important this was for Jorge. He removed a picture of himself from his wallet, and lovingly placed it inside the casket with her. After that, Jorge seemed lost forever, until death.

New Identity in Christ Jesus

How can a person overcome so much damage? How could I have rescued my son and given him what he didn't have at this time in his life? What Jorge needed was a masculine identity securely linked to the identity that only a true father can provide. How can we repair the damage that this world sometimes inflicts on a human soul? How can we reverse the damage?

One of the most amazing reasons Jesus came to earth was to bring us to the Father. It was so we could become intimately well acquainted with Father God—the Ultimate Father. Intimacy with the Father was the grandiose supernatural result of Jesus' sacrificing His life for us. He paid our ransom with His blood and rescued us from death. We were trapped in sin, in darkness, in slavery to the dominion of the flesh. We were blind, deaf, defeated and imprisoned. God the Father rescued us because He knew that nothing could satisfy the soul of man. Man must find a place where he fits, a place where he belongs, and a place where he is loved with great affection. We can conclude that the purpose behind the plan of Salvation was to bring the blind, deaf, defeated and imprisoned directly to the Heavenly Father.

I love this passage from the Book of Malachi as they are the final words God would speak to His people before the Heavens go silent for approximately 400 years. God's final words were about turning the fathers hearts to the children and the hearts of the children to the fathers, or else He would strike the land with a curse of annihilation:

"Behold, I will send you Elijah the prophet before the coming of the great and dreadful day of the LORD. And he will turn the hearts of the fathers to the children, and the hearts of the children to their fathers, lest I come and strike the earth with a curse" (Malachi 4:5-6 NKJV).

In the Book of John, we see the ultimate expression of the heart of a Father being turned toward His children when Jesus said—"I am the Way, the Truth and the Life; no one comes to the Father except through ME" (John 14:6 NKJV).

Why is so important to come to the Father? The answer is simple. Only a father can establish the identity of an individual, a true identity, a healthy identity, an identity that defines a person, and make the person whole. This assurance of who we are and assurance of self is what forms *who* we will become and how we will do it. It cannot be established or defined by a spouse, by the work we do, or by how much money we make or accumulate. Culture, tradition, religious activity, or charity work cannot establish our true identity. Though we may even offer our life to save another, it won't establish our true identity.

We cannot create our true identity ourselves. God must impart it to us. We cannot buy it because it isn't given. We cannot develop it or create it because it comes from the outside in; not from the inside out.

It is crucial for a person's optimum development to know from where he or she originates. It is vital for the soul of mankind to feel dearly loved, appreciated, and wanted. We all need to identify with someone who can teach us things we don't know, one who knows us intimately better that we know ourselves. We need a person who can tell us who we are, our innate worth; someone who can affirm us and reassure us of our unique value, and how irreplaceable we are. We need those who can guide us along the way we should go, delight in us and see our potential, our capacity, and the true purpose of our existence. Sadly, many misguided people go to psychics looking for this. Others fall into the various deceptive traps of conning others attempting to find their identity and purpose.

When I was growing up, I knew deeply how much my father loved me. He was an amazing man. I grew up confident of the worth and value I possessed. I knew there was nothing that my daddy wouldn't do for me. He would do all he could to help me understand that it was for my benefit that sometimes even included a spanking to correct me. I was confident that my father would give up his life to save mine. He was a man of honor, dignity, a man of integrity, a man of peace, a man who loved God, and I learned to trust him because he had my best interest at heart.

I greatly admire and respect him for the love and the commitment he has shown our family. My father's example made it easy for me to understand the concept of God as Father and His love. So when I introduced to Jesus Christ, I could easily accept Him as my personal Savior. I could see Him as my Father in Heaven. I understand the importance of my dad giving me his name when I was born and covering me with his firm, secure, unconditional love. As he cared for me, it was easy to understand God as a Father. Because my dad loved me, it was easy for me to accept God's gifts, promises, and unconditional love. I could appreciate His rewards and His protection when He adopted me and gave me His name. By adopting me, He made me one with Christ

(His first born), an heir of Heaven's riches and glories, a citizen of His Kingdom and all that it is in it. What a sacrifice He made, giving His Only Son to rescue and save me, and to provide me a better life here, and a future home in Heaven.

At the age of 17, with Jorge already suffering from a broken and shattered identity from a crushing father fracture, my husband George came into his life. By this time Jorge had already made so many life decisions that it seemed no matter what I would do or say, nothing could seem to change his path. He had become so emotionally guarded that he was the only one capable of protecting himself and believing in himself. Every decision he made was framed by how he felt since he relied so heavily on emotion. Living for the moment was his mantra. After all, by then that's all he felt he had. He wasn't going to trust anyone but himself and his abilities. He felt let down by men in society. He craved a father figure. A male figure in his life who would love and accept him. He also felt that life owed him, and he was going to take as much as he could from life.

Despite the desires to protect himself from rejection will deep within in his soul, Jorge kept desiring a father. He still craved a father figure yet his perspective on what a real father figure looked like had become so skewed by all the pain, rejection, and hurt. My husband George tried as much as he knew how, to show Jorge the limits, the structure, the expectations of genuine fatherly love in the life of an adult son. It was hard! George kept showing Jorge the only true way to restoration, to the wholeness of heart and forgiveness of the soul. He knew he had to make him accountable for his behavior no matter what his past had been. George knew, and had told Jorge many times, that he could rise above his past and enjoy a better future through Jesus Christ.

I never compromised with Jorge, because I knew that if he humbled himself and gave God a true, open-hearted opportunity, he would find victory. I had complete assurance and confidence knowing that the Book of Romans says, "For you did not receive the spirit of bondage again to fear, but you received the Spirit of adoption by whom we cry out, "Abba, Father" The Spirit Himself bears witness with our spirit that we are children of God…" (Romans 8:15-16 NKJV).

Run to the Father

I never stopped telling Jorge to go to the Father. Run to the Father. Hide in the Father. You can do this through Jesus Christ. The word of God tells us in the Book of Psalms (68:5) — "He is a Father to the fatherless" and (10:14) — "You are the helper of the fatherless."

In the Book of Hosea, we read that God desires sacrifices that are works of true repentance and that in the fatherless mercy will be found. (Hosea 14:2, 3) The Hebrew word for father is Abba. It's one of the first words an Israeli child learns to speak. It is translated as "daddy." Interestingly, it's this childlike word that Jesus used when referring to His Father. In Mark (14:36) we read — "…Abba, Father, all things are possible for You…"

The Holy Spirit teaches us to call God "Abba" as we saw above in Romans 8:15.

Sometimes, however, the root word "Ab" doesn't mean physical father, so much as it does "creator, builder, architect, and the one who causes something to be."

I love how King David guarded his heart and mind through the years when he was persecuted, abandoned, betrayed, and hiding alone in caves. The Book of Psalms records how David showed the trust and confidence he had in God to deliver him, to protect him and to redeem him. David knew that God was able to reestablish him, to overpower darkness on his behalf and to show him his salvation at the end.

I continually told Jorge, trust in Him, my son! The Heavenly Father will never let you down. His Word assures us that anyone who put their trust in Him will not be put to shame. (Romans 10:11) I kept reminding him that God was for us that He loves us, He will forgive us, He will receive us and He will cleanse us from all unrighteousness. I told him repeatedly that you can run to Him and He will cover you and He will protect you, and He will give you true LIFE!

When we run toward God, we must do so with a sincere heart. Otherwise, we will sabotage our blessing of running into the arms of a loving Savior. Running to God with a sincere heart is so vital because we need to come to God in genuine faith. We must approach God not looking with our physical eyes, but instead we must look with our spiritual eyes. I explained this is why the Book of Corinthians says that we walk by faith and not by sight. (2 Cor 5:7) This is why I love this Scripture from the Book of John —

"God is Spirit, and those who worship Him, most do it in spirit and in truth" (John 4:24 NKJV).

When we come to God, we don't only come to Him in adoration, respect, reverence and devotion, inspired by who He is, but we also come in spirit. Like God, we too are triune beings with spirits, souls (will, mind, emotions) and bodies. We must approach God with our heart, our true self, and we must do so in truth, meaning in the understanding of who He is. This approach will bring real, lasting change in our lives. Approaching God the Father this way will enable Him to impart His nature to us, through His presence, His character, His identity and the power of the His Holy Spirit and His gifts. Little by little we are thoroughly transformed. Approaching God and coming into His presence requires consistency, commitment, covenant, and submission.

(Author's Note: Scripture references for above statement: Deuteronomy 6:4-5, 2 Chronicles 7:14, 2 Corinthians 5:17, 1 Thessalonians 5:23, Hebrews 11:6.)

"They shall be My people, and I will be their God; then I will give them one heart and one way, that they may fear Me forever, for the good of them and their children after them. And I will make an everlasting covenant with them that I will not turn away from doing them good; but I will put My fear in their hearts so that they will not depart from Me. Yes, I will rejoice over them to do them good, and I will assuredly plant them in this land, with all My heart and with all My soul" (Jeremiah 32:38-41 NKJV).

People sometimes forget that Jesus desires to be both our Savior and our Lord. I have a special admiration for the faith and worship of Hannah in the Bible. She was supernaturally delivered from her barrenness. This is the way we all should approach God:

"And Hannah prayed and said, My heart rejoices in the Lord, my horn is exalted in the Lord. I smile at my enemies because I rejoice in Your salvation. No one is holy like the Lord, for there is none besides You, nor is there any rock like our God" (1 Samuel 2:1-2 NKJV).

When we align our faith with action, we release the power of God in us, which brings our lives into balance. The Apostle

Paul said—"When I was weak, He showed Himself strong on my behalf and within me." (2 Corinthians 12:10) Our sin nature is given no place in our lives when we have this active faith in operation.

Only God's fatherly love can truly satisfy us!

"But you are a chosen race, a royal priesthood, a dedicated nation, [God's] own purchased, special people, that you may set forth the wonderful deeds *and* display the virtues and perfections of Him Who called you out of darkness into His marvelous light. Once you were not a people [at all], but now you are God's people; once you were unpitied, but now you are pitied *and* have received mercy" (1 Peter 2:9-10 AMP).

Chapter Four
YEARS OF TORMENT

Living Between Pain and Faith

Many people have asked me how I can reconcile being a Christian and losing my son. How could a loving God allow this? My response is I would not be here today if I were not a Christian. My faith in Jesus saved my life. Does my faith exempt me from pain? No. Does my faith give me hope? Yes! I simply cannot conceive how I could even have survived the midst of the storm. I have spent countless days living between pain and faith suspended in what seems like a never-ending torrent of questions of wondering how I might have prevented it.

The reality is that the problems we face and have faced as a family is no different than those many might be facing today. We have not been exempted from problems and pain. Even for those who've not experienced a traumatic event such as the death of a child will understand the inner struggles of a faithful woman of God.

Many beautiful Christian and non-Christian homes have experienced the departure of a rebellious son or daughter; the agony of seeing one lost to drug or alcohol addiction, and feeling the desperate need to rescue them. Some have to endure their sudden horrific death from suicide, a car accident or a drug overdose. Others have lost loved ones to senseless murders that happened as a result of their being at the wrong place at the wrong time or being with the wrong crowd of people. Many times this can occur when someone has a hard-hearted and rebellious spirit borne out of a broken identity.

I sense in my heart as I begin this chapter that I should quote parts of the Book of Romans (Chapter 8). I hope that the following will be an exhortation of faith and will bring hope to you as you become a partner with me in this part of my life.

"15For (the Spirit which) you have now received (is) not a spirit of slavery to put you once more in bondage to fear, but you have received the Spirit of adoption in which we cry, Abba (Father)! Father! ... 34Who is there to condemn (us)? Will Christ Jesus (the Messiah), Who died, or rather Who was raised from the dead, Who is at the right hand of God actually pleading as He intercedes for us? ... 37Yet in all these things we are more than conquerors ... through Him, Who loved us. 38For I am persuaded beyond doubt (am sure) that neither death nor life, nor angels nor principalities, nor things impending and threatening nor things to come, nor powers, 39Nor height nor depth, nor anything else in all creation will be able to separate us from the love of God which is in Christ Jesus our Lord" (Romans 8:15, 34, 37-39 AMP).

I have felt in my Spirit that the Lord has been preparing me for this season of my life for a long time. The past nine and half years of my life have been a tremendous ride of faith and suffering for my family and me. But now that the initial trauma of the storm has passed, and the devastation has waned, the sun is dawning and a new day is breaking over the horizon. I am now confident that my Heavenly Father has equipped me to write about faith in the midst of the storm.

I know that there are many marvelously anointed preachers who share messages of success in Christ, prosperity, freedom, and healing. While those things are true, there are also trials, tribulations, troubles, temptations and the testing of our faith. I am writing this book to share with you from a broken, troubled heart; one that has experienced pain and loss.

My two boys were my life. Jorge, the eldest, was born in 1985. The younger, was born in 1995. I married my husband George in August 2002. George left for college at a young age, after giving his life to the Lord Jesus, to attend *Christ for the Nations* in Dallas, Texas. He is the one who led us to Christ.

This is my story, a story of faith in the midst of life's storms. Allow me to recap what my family and I experienced — My Son Killed Himself.

Jorge was 25 years old. He was a handsome and talented young man, remarkably smart, witty, charismatic and quite frankly he was "a mess!" Thinking about him still brings a smile to our faces. No one could make us so happy and so mad at the same time. Jorge's suicide was quite traumatic and excruciating for his younger brother, for my husband George, for my parents and many others who knew him and loved him but especially for me. The decision he made to take his life brought our family to its knees both literally and figuratively. It took us to an all-time low point and to places I could not even begin to put on the pages of this book. Life as I knew it was suddenly ripped from the center of my womb. Believe me, when a mother is wounded like this the entire foundation of the family is shaken!

How do you deal with this type of event? How do you recover and begin again when you have experienced this level of pain? After all, a broken heart is all you have left. What do you do when life as you've known it is suddenly changed forever? How do you live when one so close and so dear to your heart leaves this world by his "own" hand? How do you go on when one of those you absolutely love the most, one of those who constitutes the core and center of your world, commits suicide? What do you do then? How do you move on? You can see the world continuing to move around you, yet you are left paralyzed as if you are in a bubble where nothing moves. All that you do is breathe in pain.

I am not just talking about pain, but about all types of uninvited sorrow, calamity and suffering that come to us giving us no choice but to endure. Throughout history, humanity has faced all manner of difficulty. There have been, and will continue to be earthquakes, tsunamis, famines, injuries, revolutions, calamities, hunger, and devastation. On a personal level, we've seen division, distress, betrayal, depression, oppression, unfaithfulness, relationships that end in separation or divorce, loneliness, and fear. Additionally, there is the sense of loss of which I am familiar that comes from leaving behind a country or culture you once called home. Loss comes in many forms, shapes, and sizes, including the most terrifying of all, death!

My Testimony

As I said above, in 2002 I married a wonderful, wonderful man who knows the Lord. We married not long after we met. For our first Christmas together, I gave him an engraved bracelet that said—"To My Present from Heaven." That's what he felt like to me and my two sons. Jorge, who was turning seventeen, and my youngest who was turning seven. When my husband George came into our lives, we just knew that he was:

"A present and rescuer from Heaven", "help in the time of need", "a love so strong, holy, powerful, anointed by the Lord, chosen by Him, that could bear all things believe all things, hope all things, and overcome all things."

George truly loved and believed in God the Father, His Son and the Holy Spirit. I was moved, touched and frankly a bit troubled when I saw him talking to, living for, and trusting in "Someone" he could not see.

I had always believed God existed. But to George, God was here, now, always present, He was REAL! Soon after we were married, we began attending a church. One Sunday as I saw everyone worshiping God, the same God I thought I already knew, I decided to lift my hands in the air and close my eyes.

The Lord did not make me wait. Immediately I felt His presence and His soft voice. As soon the Pastor asked if someone wanted to come forward and accept Jesus Christ as their Lord and Savior, I walked down the aisle to receive Jesus. That day I finally got to know the Lord. I had a personal encounter with Him. After that, I was confident of these things—

- God is real and alive!
- He is God, and there is none other but Him.
- His love is unconditional.

After my personal encounter with Jesus Christ, no one could move me from this position. I quickly learned that:

"Therefore, if anyone is in Christ, he is a new creation; old things have passed away; behold, all things have become new" (2 Corinthians 5:17 NKJV).

"But if the Spirit of Him who raised Jesus from the dead dwells in you, He who raised Christ from the dead will also give life to your mortal bodies through His Spirit who dwells in you" (Romans 8:11 NKJV).

"For our citizenship is in Heaven, from which we also eagerly wait for the Savior, the Lord Jesus Christ" (Philippians 3:20 NKJV).

When I was growing up in a Catholic home, I attended a Catholic school; I lived in a culture centered on Catholicism. All of those years I practiced Christianity from the Roman Catholic point of view. I added and subtracted my sins, and tried to be a good person. I learned the basic foundations and the doctrine of the Church, the seven sacraments of the mother Church, and the five precepts that Roman Catholics are expected to follow. Meaning, I knew the dogma of the Church and respected it. I did my best to be a devoted Catholic, but that didn't work well.

When I encountered the Lord in a personal way, I yearned to know HIM, not a church. Instead, I desired nothing but Jesus Christ the Savior, God the Father and the Holy Spirit the giver of life, strength, and power. I moved forward, allowing my heart to be transformed and my mind to be renewed by His power at work within me. By learning Scripture, I found a marvelous Lord, King, Prince of Peace, Redeemer, Healer, Provider, and Rescuer.

The Holy Trinity became more real to me than I had ever known. Rather than a story that I must believe in to be Latin or Catholic, He was real. Our traditions were based on the Catholic Church since the time of the conquest of Spain, our "mother nation." I had chosen a religion to attempt to fill the void in my soul and draw me closer to God. But what I found that Sunday at that altar wasn't simply a story that you could find in a book called the "Bible." It wasn't a religious system or organization in which I needed to belong. It wasn't a religious activity to perform to feel good, or to satisfy an obligation. Instead, Christ became my truth, my everything, my personal revelation, my eternal life. I didn't depend on religious practice; suddenly I was engaged in a personal relationship with my Lord, my God, and Father.

I discovered that two things that make Christianity authentic and unique are—

First, God is directly concerned and desires to be personally involved in the lives of His children as He develops a relationship with them.

Second, there is nothing we can do to justify our salvation therefore God extends to us His grace. Mankind is incapable of meeting God's holy standards. Most beautiful of all is that our Heavenly Father has a vested interest in our good outcome, because He loves us.

Over and over again throughout Scripture God shows His love for us with vivid illustrations. We cannot even begin to comprehend the plans that God has for us and no greater is this said than in the Book of Jeremiah—

"For I know the thoughts *and* plans that I have for you, says the Lord, thoughts *and* plans for welfare *and* peace and not for evil, to give you hope in your" final outcome. Then you will call upon Me, and you will come and pray to Me, and I will hear *and* heed you. Then you will seek Me, inquire for, *and* require Me [as a vital necessity] and find Me when you search for Me with all your heart. I will be found by you, says the Lord, and I will release you from captivity…" (Jeremiah 29:11-14 AMP).

Prior to Jesus Christ coming to live in me, Scripture was boring and didn't mean as much to me. However, once I was born again, everything changed. Every truth I learned from the Word of God I began to keep as a treasure in my heart. I was different. It was as if Scripture spoke directly to me— God's Word came alive!

"But to as many as did receive *and* welcome Him, He gave the authority (power, privilege, right) to become the children of God, that is, to those who believe in (adhere to, trust in, and rely on) His name—Who owe their birth neither to bloods nor to the will of the flesh [that of physical impulse] nor to the will of man [that of a natural father], but to God. [They are born of God!]" (John 1: 12-13 AMP).

There are many devout Catholics, like my parents, for example, who know the Lord intimately and are undoubtedly saved. They read and value the Word of God because it speaks to their hearts and transforms their lives. The Charismatic movement is one of the greatest movements working inside the Catholic Church, and the Holy Spirit moves powerfully through these wonderful people! Sadly, most Catholics are little more than Sunday Catholics. The Catholic Church, Protestant Church and many mainline denominations in the U.S. lacks conviction and the power of the Holy Spirit. The Gospel of Jesus Christ has become so watered down that you will never hear the words sin, salvation or Satan. It's no wonder we are in the shape we are in as a culture.

I had to experience a profound encounter with the Almighty God to make a firm, conscious decision within my heart to believe every word of the Bible. The Bible was written under the power and anointing of the Holy Spirit by many Fathers of the faith, such as Moses, King David, Daniel, King Solomon, the Prophets, Disciples and the Apostles. All chosen by God and inspired by the Holy Spirit to bring God's revelation of Himself and His plan to mankind in the 66 books we call the Holy Bible.

Once I was born again with Jesus Christ living on the inside of me, the transformation in my life began. Though my real spiritual growth and development were under the extraordinary mentoring of a powerful man of God, Pastor Dr. John R. Counts. He encouraged, exhorted, trained, corrected, and equipped me to know who I am in Christ and who Christ is in me. I soon developed a great zeal and hunger for the Gospel. I became very strong in the Lord and my knowledge of His Word grew. I began to move by faith under the leadership of His Spirit. I was convinced that every mountain would be removed because I believed!

One of the most powerful and valuable Scriptures I learned was about the Name of Jesus—

"Therefore [because He stooped so low] God has highly exalted Him and has freely bestowed on Him the name that is above every name, That in (at) the name of Jesus every knee should (must) bow, in heaven and on earth and under the earth, And every tongue [frankly and openly] confess *and* acknowledge that Jesus Christ is Lord, to the glory of God the Father" (Philippians 2:9-11 AMP).

The Dark Side

Of course, this story has another side, the dark side. The side where the enemy (Satan) and his allies (Demons and Spirits of Darkness) dwell and mischievously devise their plans and evil intentions against us. They are determined to destroy us. They scheme, they entice, they lie, and they deceive. Jesus warned us saying, "because he (Satan) has come to steal (that which belongs to us), to destroy (the things he takes from us), and if he can, he will kill" (John 10:10). Of course we are not entirely innocent; many of us became his perfect vessels for destruction as we rebelled against God's way and authority—

"Rebellion is as the sin of witchcraft..." (1 Samuel 15:23).

"Evil people are eager for rebellion..." (Proverbs 17:11).

"If you will only obey me, you will have plenty to eat. But if you turn away and refuse to listen, you will be devoured by the sword of your enemies. I, the LORD, have spoken" (Isaiah 1:19-20 NLT).

"Don't be fooled by those who try to excuse
these sins, for the anger of God will fall on all
who disobey him" (Ephesians 5:6 NLT).

"...to obey is better than sacrifice..."
(1 Samuel 15:22).

"'What sorrow awaits my rebellious
children,' says the LORD. 'You make plans that
are contrary to mine. You make alliances not
directed by my Spirit, thus piling up your sins"
(Isaiah 30:1 NLT).

"Children, obey your parents in the Lord, for
this is right. Honor your father and mother,"
which is the first commandment with promise:
that it may be well with you and you may live
long on the earth (Ephesians 6:1-3 NKJV).

I soon learned that we are engaged in a spiritual war. The
Book of Ephesians speaks clearly about this—

"Put on God's whole armor [the armor of a
heavy-armed soldier which God supplies], that
you may be able successfully to stand up

against [all] the strategies *and* the deceits of the devil. For we are not wrestling with flesh and blood [contending only with physical opponents], but against the despotisms, against the powers, against [the master spirits who are] the world rulers of this present darkness, against the spirit forces of wickedness in the heavenly (supernatural) sphere. Therefore put on God's complete armor, that you may be able to resist *and* stand your ground on the evil day [of danger], and, having done all [the crisis demands], to stand [firmly in your place]" (Ephesians 6:11-13 AMP).

After I had been married only a few months and given my life to Christ Jesus, I began to experience this spiritual battle personally. These evil entities did not delay their appearances in our lives; they brought with them discouragement, confusion, doubt, and great challenges. They wanted to silence the Word of God that I had chosen to believe and the Word the Holy Spirit had planted in my heart. I firmly believe that Satan saw how quickly and willingly I received God's Word. Before I made one step forward in my walk with Christ, the enemy was already stealing one of my most precious possessions, and brutally attacked me. Satan despises the light of God inside us.

When I look back, I can almost see the head of darkness whispering question after question in my ears as he conspired against me. "Do you really believe God?" "Do you really trust Jesus?" "Is He really by your side?" "Is God really concerned about your interests?"

As it plotted against me, it was like darkness was saying:

"Let's see how securely this faith of yours will stand as I cast my net of schemes, and plans for destruction over you to entangle and ensnare you. I will not touch your finances (even though he did). Maybe, you will stand (I almost heard him say). I will not touch your marriage (even though he did all he could to destroy us). Perhaps you can stand (I almost heard him say).

I will not touch your body (even though he brought me to a place where I almost lost my mind). Perhaps you can stand (I almost heard him say). But I am going to attack the most valuable treasure a woman has—the fruit of your womb."

Satan knows that a mother will protect the life of her children even at the risk of her own life. Without a moment's hesitation. If it were possible for a mother to exchange her life for the life of any of her children, there would be no debate. She would gladly give her life in exchange for theirs.

In time the enemy touched, deceived, stole and destroyed the fruit of my womb, one of my dearest treasures, my firstborn son!

Decisions

Early one Saturday morning, we heard a knock on the front door and to our surprise it was the Property Manager of our apartment complex. She told us that it was very important that she speak with us, so we invited her in. To our utter dismay, she informed us that the night before there had been a huge party in one of the empty units in our apartment complex, in which Jorge was responsible. We were given two choices, neither of which were acceptable. Either, they would terminate our lease and give us two weeks to move, or they would evict Jorge. After she left our unit, my husband, and I turned to each other in shock at everything we had just heard. Immediately we asked Jorge, a senior in High School at the time, to provide us with his version of the events of what had happened the night before. He was very evasive in his answers to our questions which provided us with very little solace, security or direction as to what we should do next. Though we realized, we had no other option but to move.

Once again we sat Jorge down and told him that we would be moving. We explained that it is not because we condone or validate what he did but instead because we love him and would be giving him a second chance to prove himself. We told him that his actions were completely unacceptable and could not happen again. We explained to him that there is a reason we have established rules of the home, and he has to follow them. We establish rules in the home because we love him, and it is our responsibility as his parents to teach him. We create the framework and boundaries, and he has all the freedom to operate within those boundaries. If he chooses to go outside those boundaries, then that is when it becomes rebellion. When there is rebellion, then there will be discipline. We all understand this concept and Jorge did too.

His response, however, surprised us. He didn't respond as you would expect a typical 17-year-old to respond; emotional, reactionary or even whimsical. With a mature and charismatic demeanor he said we should not even think or consider moving as he had already been planning to leave. He told us "he was going to leave to live the life he had chosen but wasn't allowed to live in our home." He explained that he was going to be an "adult" within a few months so he should be able to live without any restrictions or accountability and should not have to answer to anybody.

We explained that life is full of restrictions and accountability and the decisions he makes at that moment will determine the rest of his life. We tried to reason with him, as we fought desperately trying to make him think about the decision he was making, but nothing worked. My husband and I were desperate. Newly married, I had just come into a personal relationship with Jesus, and already dealing with everything the gates of hell had to offer. We did not know what else to do but pray.

I continued to pray in between tears, pleading to God for my son to come to the realization of what he was planning. Suddenly just days prior to the day Jorge had committed to moving he told us that he wanted to stay. He was now willing to live within the boundaries of the home. Words cannot describe the happiness in the depths of my soul. Now my husband had to figure out what we were going to do as we only had days to find somewhere to live since we still had the ultimatum from the Property Manager. Once again all we knew to do was pray. My husband called the Property Manager, and God moved on the hearts of management and they decided to let us stay.

Our happiness didn't last as it turned into increasing sadness as many more troubling incidents with Jorge happened. Each seemed to escalate in both size and scale, including skipping school, drinking, coming home drunk and even the discovering other males spending the night. Once again we were at a crossroads. We didn't know what to do. Jorge chose not to live within the boundaries we had established for our home. When you consider we also had his seven-year-old brother to think about in every decision we made, our options were limited. My husband knew I wasn't emotionally able to make the necessary decisions either effectively or decisively. Recognizing the decisions would likely rip my heart out of my chest he told me he would make them.

My husband had unenviable decisions to make. Once again he spoke with Jorge to give him one more opportunity to see if he would choose to be a contributing member of the house but Jorge made it clear he would not. Out of options, my husband told Jorge that based on his choice to not to be a contributing member of the house; Jorge was also making a choice to enter a Non-Profit Christian facility nearby. The primary mission of the Non-Profit Christian facility was to dedicate itself to open its doors for wayward youth. He reiterated to Jorge that we love him, and ultimately this was his choice since we provided him options. Our true hope and prayer was that he would reconsider his options and make right choices after a short time at the facility. Maybe the experience based on his choice of not living with family, his mother and his brother, and the comforts of home would change his perspective. Perhaps, he would change his mind and desire to be with us. We were planning to bring him back home again under rules of love and respect towards the household and family union.

We were very worried about the possibility of Jorge making foolish decisions and throwing his life away. So, before it was time for Jorge to leave, George and I spoke with law enforcement to see what other options we might have if any. This insanity needed to stop. We explained to the police that he was threatening to leave home, and they told us that there was nothing we could do to stop him. There was nothing we could do to bring him back home if he left because he was 17 years old. The officer explained that they could help me bring him home one day, but that he could/would be gone the next if he chose. Once he turned 18, there was nothing they, nor we could do, since he would be considered an adult by the law. There was nothing I could do to save my son!

One night, just days before we were going to take him to the facility, I went into Jorge's bedroom and tried to reason with him. I sat down next to him on his bed, and I told him that George had made the decision to do whatever it would take to help him, but he must follow the rules of the home. He said no.

Despite my crying and pleading with Jorge, I couldn't make him reconsider. I was so desperate, so frustrated and so angry that I lifted my hands to shake him, to slap some sense into him. I was a desperate mother about to lose her son. Suddenly he turned and bit me in the stomach. I screamed, and George came rushing into the room. At that moment Jorge, jumped off the bed, took the phone, dialed 911, and started making wild accusations against my husband. He then threatened to accuse my husband of trying to molest him, even though I was in the room.

When the police arrived, they did not listen to us. They immediately grabbed my husband and took him like a criminal to our master bedroom to interrogate him. As soon as it was sorted out, realizing that none of which Jorge said was true, they asked if we wanted to press charges against my son. We declined. My new husband was so kind and loving with Jorge, his brother and me, and I felt so embarrassed for him that he had to endure that.

One thing I noticed, and my husband confirmed, was the spiritual darkness that kept Jorge in bondage. We found out that he had been playing with an Ouija Board for some time in his bedroom. I am not exaggerating when I say that there was a demonic presence in Jorge's room; an entity so dark and strong that I couldn't enter the house after work one day because of its presence. I called George in tears to tell him I was afraid to be in the house. George got home and cast the demonic spirits out of our apartment, and immediately, we felt a difference in the environment. I feared that these demons with whom Jorge was communicating were very powerful and were eventually going to take my son with them.

Satan's Perfect Tool

With no other options, we finally placed Jorge in the Non-Profit facility. Within three weeks he was gone, after meeting a perfect tool used by Satan. He met a young male around the same age, who befriended him and invited him to live with him and a much older attorney in a luxurious apartment complex in Houston. This attorney would attract and corrupt teenagers, introduce them to a lifestyle of drugs and worldly pleasure while destroying their future. It wasn't long before Jorge was blinded by drugs, alcohol and all types of excess. He became very selfish and increasingly rebellious. Life for us had now become a living hell.

Jorge was extremely handsome and charming, and older men would take him shopping at the most expensive designer stores, to wild upscale parties, to flaunt their extravagant lifestyle. I will never be able to forget how quickly and fully sin can consume a person, even to one's ultimate destruction.

Those who knew Jorge understood that he was very vulnerable and broken having been rejected by his birth father. He wanted to know his father to understand his own identity. He sought reconciliation and acceptance but instead found rejection. He desperately wanted to forge a bond but instead was broken in pieces. Out of the rejection of his father he never came to know who he was because he never discovered whose he was. His identity obliterated.

Jorge was emotionally handicapped by the abuse and mistreatment by father figures and "heroes" in his life during his formative years. Then the death of Mami a few months before all these events started taking place completely shattered Jorge. With a fractured identity, Jorge was easy prey for Satan and these newly identified father figures who would come to him and offer him all the world has to offer.

Not long after, Jorge met a man named Charlie* (name changed) nearly 15 years his elder who supported Jorge financially for nearly nine years. Within Jorge's circle of friends, he came to be widely known as Jorge's "Sugar Daddy." Charlie gave him all the money he needed to live very comfortably, with little to no responsibilities. The emotional crutch this man provided, encouraged Jorge to gratify himself in a fantasy, but the fantasy became Jorge's reality, and in the end, his destruction.

I cannot tell you all the remaining things that happened because it is such a long story with many years of excruciating pain. The next seven years of Jorge's life where shrouded in secrecy. I didn't know my son's address, if he was sick, hungry, or even if he was dead or alive. We never met Charlie, but we only knew the things Jorge and his friends would say about him. We would go month after month without a word from Jorge. Then I would learn he was alive because out of nowhere he would call me to meet him. The silence was deafening. The pain of the unknown was excruciating.

I felt so isolated and alone in my despair. There was nothing my husband could do. He reminded me that we couldn't save someone who didn't want to be saved. Ultimately all Jorge wanted was to live the life he had chosen. As painful as the words were, I knew in my heart that what George said was true.

Losing My Son

One night, a few years after Jorge left the house, he attempted to commit suicide. There may have been others, but this was the only time of which I was aware. He took a bottle of pills and then called me to say goodbye. I begged him to call 911 immediately because it was clear that he was under the influence of drugs with alcohol.

Names of God

In the middle of the night, the EMT's (Emergency Medical Technicians) went to his rescue as we raced to the hospital. I

91

remember that night so vividly. I was pleading with God to stop his premature death because my Jorge had not come into a personal relationship with Jesus Christ.

I remember calling on the name of Jehovah-El-Shaddai, which means "God-Almighty." (Genesis 17:13) This name of God emphasizes His ability to handle any situation that confronts His people. He is able to deal victoriously and to devastate His enemies.

In the car on our way to the hospital, I called aloud to Jehovah-Nissi, which means the "Lord is my Conqueror, my Banner, and my Victory." (Exodus 17:15-16) When all seems lost at the hands of our enemies, and we lift our hands and surrender all to our Lord, He will come to our rescue and defeat our enemies.

I went on and called on the name of Jehovah-Shamah, which means the "Lord is there." (Ezekiel 48:35) The Lord is omniscient—ever-present!

I cried out in the car to Jehovah-Ropheka, "The Lord is my Healer." (Exodus 15:26) I asked, interceded and pled as a child of the Living Holy One, in Jesus Name, for God to show up on my and my son's behalf—and He did!

Once again Father God showed up on my behalf to prevent Satan from overwhelming us. We arrived at the hospital, and the doctors told us that he would be okay. Once Jorge was released from the hospital, we brought him to our house. While he recovered there, we proposed a new idea to him as we knew he needed to be far away from all of the terrible influences in his life in Houston.

My husband knew about an amazing place in Los Angeles called The Dream Center, a ministry where Jorge could find healing inside and out. At The Dream Center, many lost individuals have found themselves, and in the process, have found Jesus Christ. A person usually stays there for a year or more and are introduced to life as God intended them to live. You can find more information at www.dreamcenter.org.

When we initially inquired, the Dream Center was filled, and they had no space for anyone else. George spoke with the one of the Directors of this amazing ministry, and they allowed Jorge to enroll immediately. We quickly purchased an airline ticket, and my husband put Jorge on a plane to Los Angeles. I was so thankful for this opportunity given to Jorge and so full of hope he would see reality. However, through no fault of the Dream Center, Jorge only stayed there one night, as it is totally voluntary.

Jorge returned to Houston, determined that he was not going to stay in Los Angeles. He said he wanted to be back home with us, but after speaking with him we were not convinced that he had any intention of leaving his previous lifestyle behind. A lifestyle of an excess of every kind that took him to the verge of death. A lifestyle that we could not and would not allow any exposure or influence for his young brother. We truly believed that the Dream Center was the best place for him. Jorge did not agree.

I couldn't find anyone who could help me rescue my son and bring him home to me. My son wasn't ready to obey the rules of our house, to abide by our standards of sobriety, and commit to living as a responsible young adult. No one could help us because Jorge wasn't willing to help himself. All I had to rely on was this newly-revealed faith in Jesus Christ.

Growing in Christ

During that time, we were attending a Bible Study on Monday Night's led by Pastor Dr. John R. Counts. These Bible Studies helped equip me to deal with every circumstance that life could bring me. One night after one of our studies, the owner of the home where it was being held told me, "Jessica, don't give up, my darling. The Bible tells us in Acts 16:31, "believe in the Lord Jesus and you will be saved along with everyone in your household." It was as if the Heavens opened for me when I heard those words.

On another occasion, during the same Bible study, I read the words of the prophet Isaiah, who said:

> "The Spirit of the Lord God is upon me, because the Lord has anointed *and* qualified me to preach the Gospel *of* good tidings to the meek, the poor, *and* afflicted; He has sent me to bind up *and* heal the brokenhearted, to proclaim liberty to the [physical and spiritual] captives and the opening of the prison *and* of the eyes to

those who are bound, To proclaim the acceptable year of the Lord [the year of His favor]...to comfort all who mourn" (Isaiah 61:1-2 AMP).

I remembered feeling strong and empowered again, with one more promise in my favor. The Messiah was going to release the captives! I immediately started to meditate once again on the fact that the Lord was my answer because the Lord is our answer. There is no area of our lives that He can't improve when we give Him access to it.

Today, many are unfamiliar with the term "covenant" as they have no understanding of what a true covenant is. The Latin word for covenant is "testament." A true covenant is a pact or a contract between two parties which is not to be broken. When we enter into a covenant with a person, or with God, the covenant itself details the terms of the agreement. When the Lord God is one of the parties in a covenant, He will certainly fulfill His part of the agreement, no question about it. Because I entered into a personal relationship with Jesus Christ I can have confidence that He will fulfill His end of the covenant with me. In the Book of Hebrews, it says that Jesus is the Mediator of a better Covenant which was established on better promises. (Hebrews 8:6). Jesus facilitated a better covenant with better promises because of the blood He shed on the cross for us. That is God's covenant with us.

Listen to these beautiful words in the Book of Psalms:

> "Though I walk in the midst of trouble, You will revive me; You will stretch forth Your hand against the wrath of my enemies, and Your right hand will save me. The Lord will accomplish what concerns me; Your lovingkindness is forever; do not forsake the works of Your hands" (Psalms 138:7-8 NASB).

I began to see the pieces come together, understanding that the only hope I had to rescue my son was God. God was the way. His power is endless. I became compelled to know Christ more fully. I fell in love with Him and meditated on His Word day and night, growing in knowledge and faith.

Among many Scriptures I learned, and love are:

> "[God] disarmed the principalities and powers that were ranged against us and made a bold display *and* public example of them, in triumphing over them in Him *and* in it [the cross]" (Colossians 2:15 AMP).

> "But God, who is rich in mercy, because of His great love with which He loved us, even when we were dead in trespasses, made us alive

together with Christ (by grace you have been saved), and raised us up together, and made us sit together in the Heavenly places in Christ Jesus, that in the ages to come He might show the exceeding riches of His grace in His kindness toward us in Christ Jesus. For by grace, you have been saved through faith, and that not of yourselves; it is the gift of God" (Ephesians 2:4-8 NKJV).

Soon, I learned about the power that is in Christ Jesus. It includes the power of His Name, the power of His blood, the power of His authority and dominion over darkness. I learned about faith by reading His Word daily, listening to Scripture daily, spending time in His presence and even reading amazing books about faith and spiritual warfare. I was excited about the Lord, and I was confident that He alone has the victory over death, hell, and the grave.

"Your word is a lamp to my feet and a light for my path" (Psalm 119:105 NKJV).

"And Jesus answered them, Truly I say to you, if you have faith (a firm relying trust) and do not doubt, you will not only do what has been done to the fig tree, but even if you say to this mountain, Be taken up and cast into the sea, it will be done. And whatever you ask for in prayer, having faith *and* [really] believing, you will receive" (Matthew 21: 21-22 AMP).

"Jesus said to him, If you can believe, all things are possible to him who believes" (Mark 9:23 NKJV).

Exercising Faith

Many times my husband would come home and find me praying and crying out of my frustration as I worshiped the Lord. I will never forget the day when George told me, "Baby, your tears alone will not move the hand of God, your faith will! This is not to say that God does not see our tears or that He is not a God of compassion, but our faith moves God."

According to the Book of Hebrews—

"But without faith it is impossible to please *and* be satisfactory to Him. For whoever would come near to God must [necessarily] believe that God exists and that He is the rewarder of those who earnestly *and* diligently seek Him [out]" (Hebrews 11:6 AMP).

On that day, I reconsidered what true faith was. Real faith is a confident reliance on someone who is faithful, able and just. One of the toughest challenges of my life was to release my son and my problems to God. Could I fully trust and rely on Him? One night I closed the door to my room and knelt down to honor God. I placed both of my hands on my womb and offered it to God. It was as if I'd stripped it from inside me and offered it up to Heaven. I cried out, saying:

"LORD, I GIVE YOU THE FIRSTFRUIT OF MY WOMB! I know that he is dirty, unworthy of you, maybe he is of no value at all right now as he is; but please take him, take him. (My arms trembled, trying to reach the sky.) I give you custody of my first born son my child. I have no one but You, Lord. Do not reject my first born son. I am convinced that your love for him is much larger and stronger than mine. Your desire for his salvation is more powerful and stronger than mine. I know you love him. You gave your Only Son to rescue him. Please take custody of my son, Lord. Go to the places I cannot go. Be present there when I cannot be. Speak to him when I have no voice. Touch him when I am too far away. Save him, Lord. I cannot do anything at all."

I was especially comforted when I read these words in the Book of Hebrews:

"Inasmuch then as we have a great High Priest Who has [already] ascended *and* passed through the heavens, Jesus the Son of God, let us hold fast our confession [of faith in Him]. For we do not have a High Priest Who is unable to understand *and* sympathize *and* have a shared feeling with our weaknesses *and* infirmities *and* liability to the assaults of temptation, but One Who has been tempted in every respect as we are, yet without sinning. Let us then fearlessly *and* confidently *and* boldly draw near to the throne of grace (the throne of God's unmerited favor to us sinners), that we may receive mercy [for our failures] and find grace to help in good time for every need [appropriate help and well-timed help, coming just when we need it]" (Hebrews 4:14-16 AMP).

I knew the Blood of Christ covered me. I began to enter His presence with words of worship and adoration, just as the four living creatures in Heaven do. (Revelation 4:8) In a resounding chorus with His saints who are there right now, I began to proclaim God's glory, splendor, power, and grace. I entered God's sanctuary near the throne of God through the torn veil that is the flesh of Jesus Christ in intimate intercessory prayer. (Hebrews 10:19-22), I was confident I would find the help and mercy that only God my Father could provide. I knew that every time I entered I was entering through the torn flesh of Jesus Christ and His blood would saturate me and cover me completely. God is so amazing.

I was also aware that the accuser (Satan) of the brethren was also there making false charges against my son, even as I sought his salvation. I did this will full confidence that I had overcome the devil by the Blood of Jesus Christ and the word of my testimony. (Revelation 12:10-11)

I learned to fight the good fight of faith. Spiritual warfare became my area of accomplishment and knowledge. I fought others' battles and saw them obtain their victories. George and I also obtained victory in many areas of our lives too.

In general, I've had several years of significant spiritual victories, aside from my son's tragic death. Through it all, I have learned to have joy and to be content, living day by day by faith.

As far as my son was concerned, I worshiped and prayed, and I fervently interceded for him. I learned to take the authority God has given us to restrain the devil, and to cancel the terrible plots the enemy formed against my son, Jorge. In the Spirit, I restricted their power and dominion over him. I claimed that the seed of the righteous will be delivered! (Proverbs 11:21) I stood on the fact that no weapon formed was going to prosper against the house of the righteous. In

Exodus 20:6 the Lord declares that He will have mercy and compassion, and will extend much grace to the descendants of His faithful ones; those who love Him and Keep His Commandments. I learned to walk by faith and not by sight. In short, I learned the reality of what we find in James 5:16: "The prayer of a righteous person accomplishes much."

The years flew by so quickly. I had a good job with a great company, and family and friends who loved me. I needed constant reminders that regardless of Jorge's condition, I was responsible to be cheerful and enjoy life with those around me. At times, it was difficult to maintain my trust, faith, and soundness of mind in the midst of my circumstances. But I was aware that according to James 1:8, a double-minded person is unstable in all his ways. I had to keep guard over my heart.

There were multiple occasions on which my son took more than a lethal dose of drugs that could have killed him. However, I am convinced that based on the covenant with us, the Lord was faithful to restrain Jorge from dying because he wasn't saved. I am confident in this after what I discovered when Jorge had returned from a period in which he lived in Miami (not to be confused with the time his father rejected him). He told me that he had been hospitalized multiple times as a result of attempting to commit suicide.

On one of those occasions, after becoming unconscious from a drug overdose, he said he heard a voice calling his name. He told me he saw Jesus standing in the room. Although he was somewhat incoherent, Jesus said to him,

"Get up, take your clothes and leave. If you don't, you will die." After that incident, when Jorge would fall asleep again, he would wake up quickly. That experience so terrified him that when he returned to Houston, he never touched cocaine or any other illicit drugs again. This was nothing short of a Heavenly intervention. He was set free from his addiction, and he was so happy! For years afterward, I was able to enjoy my son again. The final two or three years of his life we were finally able to enjoy being with him, and to spend time with him. When I looked into his eyes, it was clear that my real son was back!

My Son Killed Himself

Chapter Five
COMING BACK
(THE LAST YEAR)

The apostle Paul writes:

"The saying is sure and true and worthy of full universal acceptance, that Christ Jesus (the Messiah) came into the world to save sinners, of whom I am foremost" (1 Timothy 1:15 AMP).

The apostle Peter reminds us:

"He personally bore our sins in His [own] body on the tree [as on an altar and offered Himself on it], that we might die (cease to exist) to sin and live to righteousness. By His wounds you have been healed" (1 Peter 2:24 AMP).

James records:

"You believe that there is one God. You do well. Even the demons believe and tremble" (James 2:19 NKJV).

We were so happy the last year of Jorge's life and I can't help but bless the Lord that I had an opportunity to get so close to Jorge once again. Three years had passed since deliverance and departure from illicit drugs. We saw each other quite often and spent Thanksgiving, Christmas, and birthdays together.

When 2010 arrived, it just felt different. Jorge seemed to have had an epiphany and had matured. We had fewer disagreements, and he was focusing on trying to start a company of his own. He seemed to be more settled. We felt that he had learned from his past mistakes and was now becoming responsible and more self-sufficient.

Once again we were able to share in his laughter and enjoy his charming, bubbling and charismatic personality. At the beginning of 2011 we even had the incredible joy of being with him for his younger brother's 16th birthday. Jorge and I cooked his brother's favorite casserole together, and Jorge spent the night with us. As we all sang "Happy Birthday" to his brother we felt complete. A family again! I was ecstatic. Words cannot describe how happy I was!

Each day I would call him as I left work, and we would just talk about the other's day. We typically made plans to see each other on Saturdays, and slowly I began to feel whole again. On the surface, all appeared to be going well. During this time, Jorge had been seeing Dr. Red, a lovely man, mentor, and counselor. I greatly respected him as I had met him shortly after I came to the United States, and he had been a major pillar in my life for the previous 16 years. He gave me guidance, a sense of security and was like a father figure to me as my family was in Central America. I learned to rely upon his wise counsel. I was thrilled to know that Jorge was now seeing him. It seemed that Jorge was making significant progress. Little did we know that there were other events happening simultaneously in Jorge's life; events that would bring us to the final round of the fight for his life.

During Jorge's visits with Dr. Red, Jorge began to review and relive his childhood and teenage years. They discussed the effects that drugs, alcohol, and the immorality of living a homosexual lifestyle had on his relationship with his family. We began to see tremendous improvement. However, there were areas where Dr. Red was not able to gain much traction; specifically as it related to Jorge fully understanding the consequences of his decisions. You see, Jorge had grandiose visions and unrealistic dreams and expectations. He was never content merely being normal or average. Instead, he wanted everything, and he wanted it now. It was as if Jorge had a debt with life and he wanted to take all he could from his damaged position. Jorge became consumed with greed and sense of entitlement. They were his attempt to fill the voids in his heart from feelings of rejection, abandonment, a troubled and confused mind—all which only the Lord Jesus can fill. Without God's active Word taking root in our minds, and our submission to His authority, we will not find true stability or peace. We will remain at the mercy of our fractured self-identity.

One of the main areas I underestimated was Jorge's history of drug use. The drugs took a terrible toll on his mind. He was delusional. He lived in a "fantasy land," and suffered from delusions of grandiosity, which some experts feel is a form of Schizophrenia. With Jorge's high IQ and his charismatic charm, he somehow managed to deceive us all. However, the person wrapped in the greatest deception was Jorge himself.

He was becoming more and more obsessed with living a lifestyle of the rich and famous, yet we were not cognizant of this due to patient/doctor confidentiality. The irony of all was that Dr. Red even wanted to believe him and hoped for the best outcome. We hoped that Jorge wanted to exchange the evil for good, his pain for joy, and his losses for gains. Once again, only the Lord Jesus can perform that type of work inside a man or woman, assuming the man or woman allows God to perform the work.

It seems that Jorge was adamant to demonstrate that he could do something worthwhile with his life. Though we knew that only Jesus our Hope of Glory within could truly reestablish him and our family. (Colossians 1:27)

Before the craziness started and shortly after my divorce, Jorge was excited to be working as a teenager. He was hired to work as a host in a restaurant and worked very hard. He was also quite generous. Each week for a year he gave me his check so that I could do the grocery shopping for him, his brother, and me. But it didn't take long for drugs, the filthy world and everything that comes with it, to rob him of his honor and dignity.

It became obvious that much of Jorge's life was becoming veiled in secrecy. He had developed financial survival skills, and we couldn't rely on the accuracy of his stories.

At the beginning of 2010, we were told that Jorge's "special friend" Charlie, became quite ill due to his heavy use of alcohol, drugs, and homosexual promiscuity. Needless to say, this relationship with Charlie was always a point of great conflict between the two of us and clearly I could never see right motives. The mother's heart in me sees a predator exposing the fragile nature of broken identity of my son. I had come to discover he was in Jorge's life since he was 17 years old directing his path and reaffirming in him everything contrary to our position. I would like to clarify that Jorge's autopsy revealed that he did not have HIV or AIDS.

When Jorge learned about Charlie's condition, he started taking care of him, even though they weren't living in the same house. We did not know how much things would once again change.

Not long after that, Jorge called to tell me that he was once again moving. We had become quite accustomed to Jorge moving as he did so quite frequently. Somehow he always managed to live in the best places in town but this time was different. Gone were the high-rise apartments, condos, and lofts. Instead, Jorge moved into a brand new, nearly million dollar home located in a well-known upper-class Houston neighborhood. When he told me he was leasing to buy, and he had paid up to six months in advance, I was in shock. Once he moved in, he invited me over to see the house.

When I arrived, I was immediately struck by the sheer number of people who were leisurely coming and going to the house. Jorge seemed to be supporting a large number of people there, and some were even living there. I told Jorge that they were like leeches, as most of them did not work to support themselves. I have a sarcastic and painful smile on my face today when I think about those words. We mothers can be extremely naive about our kids. Jorge himself had lived off others for years as well. He believed with true conviction that all these people cared for him. When he became aware of the truth that they did not, he was totally devastated.

As Jorge began to take me on a tour of the house, I was immediately overtaken by an incredible and overwhelming sense of sadness. I knew in my heart that nothing is free in life, and somehow this wasn't good. George and I interrogated him as much as we could about this new life he was living, but we couldn't seem to get through to him, or getting the truth from him. Quite frankly, many times it was easier to accept what he said and give him the benefit of the doubt, even though we knew something wasn't right. The constant battle of trying to pry the truth out of him, while pointing him to the Truth (Jesus) left us exhausted. (John 14:6)

At this point, my husband George became the main person to mitigate the damage Jorge's habits and lies could have on his brother and me. It was very difficult for George to continue being the dam that constantly restrained the water from flooding our emotions. George could not afford to let his guard down. Constantly mitigating the damage, restraining the water while knowing the path Jorge was walking down left him devastated and crushed. He loved Jorge like a son, but he had to make hard decisions; decisions that were in everyone's best interest, not just Jorge's. Creating a constant bone of contention between the two of them. As Jorge's mom, it was quite difficult for me. His brother became our focus as we both sought to shelter him from Jorge's stupidity and immorality.

One night I almost lost both of my sons at the same time; one could have been in jail for life and the other, dead from alcohol poisoning. Without our knowledge, one afternoon Jorge took his 13-year-old brother, to spend time with him and his friends. Jorge and his friends began giving his brother alcohol without stopping. His brother had never touched it before in his life. He became so drunk that he almost died from alcohol poisoning. This was commonplace in the lifestyle Jorge was living with his friends. To say that we were livid is an understatement.

More than ever we realized that we could not take things with Jorge, at face value though instinctively we always knew this. Even though things might have appeared "normal" on the surface, we knew that with Jorge, nothing was ever as it seemed. We immediately begin to prepare ourselves to deal with whatever consequences Jorge's new lifestyle would bring him, and the devastation that would accompany it. My husband knew that one day Jorge would regret the choices he was making, and would eventually bring me pain and devastation, from which he was always trying to protect us.

We took slight consolation in that we were always told that Charlie was very wealthy which gave us a glimmer of hope that maybe things were as Jorge said. To this day, we still don't know the truth, although that matters little when you have lost your son.

During this time, I kept hearing screams inside my heart saying that all is not well and that soon my son would be gone. I cannot explain these ominous feelings. Many times I felt I was losing my mind. Feelings of pure desperation, like I had never known, would grip me, and seemingly not let go. The fear that I might not be able to save my son haunted me. I couldn't find a way to give voice to these cries, or to articulate them. I knew so clearly what the Book of Proverbs said:

> "Satisfied desire is sweet to a person; therefore it is hateful *and* exceedingly offensive to [self-confident] fools to give up evil [upon which they have set their hearts]" (Proverbs 13:19 AMP).

As time passed, the intensity of these feelings increased. It was horrendous. I tried to explain it to my mother, my aunt (mom's sister), and to my brother as a sense of being on a roller coaster. The coaster takes you slowly and steadily up to the highest point. Then suddenly, as you see the clear blue sky and begin to relax, you are met with the sickening feeling that it's over, and you begin a terrifying unstoppable and rapid descent.

We were so confused about how to address all of these new events in Jorge's life. Equally puzzling, we had no idea how to deal with Jorge's overnight affluence. Since Charlie had come into Jorge's life at 17, we never saw him lack anything. On other occasions, Jorge moved to South Beach with a few older men who became his benefactors. Most of Jorge's friends agreed with me that young, attractive kids are lured and enticed into this lifestyle through charm, expensive gifts, and extravagant habits. One of the unspoken truths and politically incorrect truths about the homosexual lifestyle is that promiscuity is at the highest levels. It is well-known by doctors, psychologists, and therapists that the number of one's sexual partners can go into the hundreds. Although there are exceptions, behind the scenes, many live emotionally devastated due to the consequences. The homosexual lifestyle is not as Hollywood often embellishes it. It is often a life filled with loneliness, pain, anger, and despair.

Almost every Saturday I went to see Jorge. As difficult as it sometimes was, I felt blessed to be able to spend time with him. My mind goes back to one night in particular when I was visiting him. He hid my purse, called my husband and told him jokingly that he was "kidnapping" me and one of his friends mothers for the night so that we could spend the night with them. We all left for what I thought was dinner, and we ended up in a gay nightclub, and I cannot describe what I saw that night. When I was single, and before I had accepted Christ, I was familiar with "clubbing." However, what I saw that night, in that club, was nothing like I had ever seen in my entire life including when I was going out "clubbing" in the past and dancing.

Sadly, I never really got to spend much time with him that night because all of his "friends" were around him. Each of them had an agenda living the life that Jorge provided for them. Jorge bought everything. Shots of liquor and other drinks flowed nonstop. He held nothing back, monetarily speaking, from his mob of "friends." They became more insatiable for the money, shopping sprees at the most expensive stores, and for the riches that they were being provided. What could I say, Jorge was living the same way, from someone else's resources. The saddest part to me was that all Jorge seemed to want in return was their validation, companionship, family bonds, and to feel glorified and adored by them.

Jorge wanted to feel worthy. He sought that worth and value in the adoration of his friends. How sad is that? That can't come from man. Only the Lord can provide us with a true sense of worth.

"Thus says the Lord: Cursed is the man who trusts in man and makes flesh his strength, whose heart departs from the Lord" (Jeremiah 17:5 NKJV).

During this time, I observed that Jorge was trying very hard to start three different businesses and was excited to think that he was going to make it this time and become truly independent. Jorge tried so hard to reestablish himself, but he never surrendered his mind to the Lord. He had hired many "friends" to work for him in many different capacities. He hired his friends to work for him as personal assistants, business development, and marketing specialist positions to help grow the business. In the end, it was very clear they didn't do any of that.

One of the business ventures Jorge was most excited about was the prospect of opening a restaurant; but I told him that things were not favorable for this, and he quickly discovered that "mama was right." When the money ran out, and all of his "friends" were gone; as quickly and suddenly as it had started, the fantasy was over! His "friends" stole all they could, and then they vanished as quickly as the money.

For the wisdom of this world is foolishness to God. As the Scripture says, "He traps the wise in the snare of their own cleverness." And again, "the Lord knows the thoughts of the wise; He knows they are worthless" (1 Corinthians 3:19-20).

I might add that during this time of "fantasy," Jorge did seem to help many people who came to him asking for financial help. Even when the economy collapsed, I was told that Jorge somehow managed to help save more than one person from a home foreclosure. I heard about others who Jorge provided a car to commute to college and to pay their bills. Jorge had a kind and generous heart. Sin blinds, misleads, and corrupts the mind, will, and emotions of man.

The Crossroads of Christ

Many times Jorge would get angry at me because of my way of thinking, and my stand against what I knew to be shameful, exceedingly immoral and inappropriate behavior. Many times, I spoke openly about this with both Jorge and his "friends" holding nothing back; although I did it with love and sincerity. Jorge's friends knew that I honestly cared for them, and I had no "hidden agenda."

My honesty and sincerity did not come without consequences; a place my husband defines as "The Crossroads of Christ." The place where our will and desires intersect with the cross of Christ. All of us will be at the crossroads where we are forced to choose—will we choose to follow the will of Jesus Christ or will we choose to follow the will of Satan?

We have no greater example than Jesus presenting this exact choice to His disciples:

> "Then Jesus said to His disciples, If anyone desires to be My disciple, let him deny himself [disregard, lose sight of, and forget himself and

his own interests] and take up his cross and follow Me [cleave steadfastly to Me, conform wholly to My example in living and, if need be, in dying, also]. For whoever is bent on saving his [temporal] life [his comfort and security here] shall lose it [eternal life]; and whoever loses his life [his comfort and security here] for My sake shall find it [life everlasting]" (Matthew 16:24-25 AMP).

Many times I would stand at the crossroads of Christ, forced to stand strong—choosing either a relationship with my son or selling out my values, convictions, and beliefs. You see Jorge would threaten to never speak to me or see me again if I did not fully accept and embrace his lifestyle and "life partner." I loved my son with everything in me, but I could not accept these "terms" he was demanding. It was my love for him and the fact that I cared for many of his friends that compelled me to tell them the truth. For the same reason, Jesus and the apostles were killed. I wasn't willing to dismiss the significance of the Cross of Christ to maintain a close relationship with my son. Likewise, I wasn't planning to go to the next Gay Pride Parade while holding a rainbow flag just to satisfy and make peace with him. Nor would I do it out of false guilt either. After all, if his *newly discovered convictions* are worthy of respect then most assuredly, mine are as well as they have been for two thousand years.

My love for my son wasn't going to change nor could I allow it to modify, change or annul God's Word. Once the cross of Christ awakened me, I realized that genuine love compels a believer to encourage people to become their best through Jesus Christ, our Hope of Glory.

I knew that my spirit had been born of God and not of man (John 1:13). I also knew that one day the Gospel of Christ would resonate in Jorge's head and heart to the point that he too would surrender his will. I knew that if Jorge allowed it, God would transform him and bring him into complete reconciliation with Jesus Christ. However, true salvation requires repentance. These days it is popular to teach a path to salvation without even mentioning repentance from sin. A message of salvation without repentance is a heinous deception. True salvation cannot occur without repentance, and repentance cannot take place until we acknowledge our sin.

Jorge wanted me and my family, to embrace his homosexual lifestyle and all that came with it; including the acceptance of his future "marriage" to his life-partner and their desire to adopt a child. We were always clear that we would not do so. We knew that by accepting it, we would be validating it. I loved and adored Jorge to my core, but I could not validate, embrace or affirm his lifestyle. Where has this lie come from that to *love* somebody, we must embrace their sexual orientation? I can love my son without loving his choices. To conflate the two issues is deception, and it has overtaken our culture and has overtaken the church.

God created the family structure as one man and one woman for a reason. I am convinced that anything contrary to that is contrary to God's word. When we embrace anything outside of God's word, it will have dire consequences and repercussions on our society, both today and in the years to follow. We already have enough on our plate with blended families, stepmoms, and stepdads.

One of the arguments on this topic is always, are you saying that that gays cannot be good parents? No, I am not saying that. Can they not have good values and morals? I believe that they can be very good, nice and lovely people. My answer to this is based on the same faulty foundation — *Sin*. I am not here to evaluate man's standards and values. This story is about God's ways, not man's ways; God's standards of love, family, and marriage; not man's. We have all proven how wrong we are without the indwelling Christ in our lives. I am not referring to human morality. I am referring to the morality produced when we allow Christ Jesus to be Lord of our lives, which is evidenced by obedience.

In today's "politically correct" world, the position we took and are taking isn't popular nor readily accepted. However, my primary concern is not what is popular with society, but what is acceptable to God. Many times I looked right into my son's eyes, and I told him, "Jorge, I love you with all of my heart, and nothing will change that. Acceptance? I have accepted you since the moment you were an embryo growing inside me. However, I will not accept the lifestyle you are choosing because it is wrong, period." Radical? Yes. It's as radical as one can be. It's a matter of right from wrong.

Typically this would make him furious with me, and he would accuse me of being stubborn and close-minded. I would reply, "Not really, my mind is open for you because I love you. My mind is open for you to live the life God intends for you, not the deception that this world wants to put in your head. God intends for you to live the holy life He desires." Should I rely on society's views, changing concepts, and agendas? No way!

The world has proven from the beginning that without Christ, we are subject to our continually changing hearts and minds. What is wonderful and truth today was error yesterday. What is normal today, was abnormal yesterday. What is law and love, depending on culture, race and creed today, can be wrong tomorrow. Why would I place my trust in man's emotions, ambitions, and agendas?

On many occasions, I took the same position with some of Jorge's closest friends. I would tell them, "Maybe the world is telling you that the lifestyle of homosexuality is normal and that there is nothing wrong with it. I am telling you that it's not good, it's not normal, or natural. With the same passion that this world tells you that you have the right to live this lifestyle, I encourage you to live the life that God planned for you. You have the right to be in a relationship with a female, and a right to establish a family where a mother and father are the foundations of the home. You, as a husband, in a union with a God-given wife, one who is naturally equipped to procreate with you, can share the pleasure of your children! Yes, you can have it all, and be happy, and fulfill God's desire for you which is holiness."

You have no idea how many desire to hear these words. Instead, most Christians are disinterested, immobilized, fearful or most likely telling them that it is fine to continue doing what they are doing, which is sin. We cannot be a light in the darkness as long as we cower down, afraid of what people think of us. But I will pose a question to you. Do you think that the ones who are aggressively pushing the LGBT agenda have any intention of stopping or backing down?

To those who are engaged in this lifestyle, Christ and His Cross and its transforming power passionately say to you:

"Stop deceiving yourselves. If you think you are wise by this world's standards, you need to become a fool to be truly wise" (1 Corinthians 3:18 NLT).

"The message of the cross is foolish to those who are headed for destruction! But we who are being saved know it is the very power of God" (1 Corinthians 1:18 NLT).

Stronghold

What is a stronghold? A stronghold is a fortified area of deception that takes root in our soul (will, mind, emotions) in which we become convinced we cannot overcome. Strongholds when established in our soul take root and produce actions and reactions in our heart according to what we perceive to be true. Many strongholds are born out of fear of pain and rejection (emotional and physical) that was inflicted in our past, especially our childhood. God has a remedy for these strongholds. I don't boast to you that I am completely free of sin, or from emotional captivity. I too have been captive to many of them in the past:

> "For though we walk in the flesh, we do not war according to the flesh, for the weapons of our warfare are not of the flesh, but divinely powerful for the destruction of fortresses. We are destroying speculations and every lofty thing raised up against the knowledge of God, and we are taking every thought captive to the obedience of Christ" (2 Corinthians 10:3-5 NASB).

Allow me to clarify something I believe beneficial for both you and me. Homosexuality is a stronghold rooted in the soul of a man or a woman who has a broken identity. It resolves nothing. Instead, it perpetuates even more conflicted emotions. Jorge struggled with these emotional conflicts every day and was unable to overcome them until the end of his life. There are several wonderful support groups of ex-lesbians and ex-gays that offer hope to those trapped in this lifestyle. Many of them are successfully married today. Healing and help are available. I recommend a couple of the following websites:

- www.pfox.org
- www.joedallas.com

My purpose for this book is not to focus on the homosexual lifestyle or to cast shame on persons engaged in that lifestyle. I do not abhor, or dislike anyone involved in that lifestyle. I care for and honestly love them as I love others, with the love of Christ. However, with Jorge so bound by it, for me to eliminate it from the equation would not be appropriate nor can I.

In Jorge's most vulnerable and intimate moments with me, he told me that he didn't believe in homosexuality, and even less in the lesbian lifestyle. He even told a few of his friends the same thing, even though he had a maintained an external façade. He fought strongly for it because it had become his identity.

I am not declaring with 100% certainty the death of my son to be due to homosexuality. However, I can't say with 100% certainty that the death of my son is not due to homosexuality? The gay agenda would say that the death of my son is because we did not embrace his homosexuality and because of this he felt rejected and unaccepted. We cannot continue using the mantra of rejection or acceptance to explain the rate of suicide within that community. I continually assured Jorge that I would love him always because he was my son and that we always accepted him. Although, I would not accept his lifestyle. I am familiar with the torment these conflicting desires seem to cause so many including my son yet I will not connect the dots to say that these same conflicts contributed to his decision to take his life. I contend that anyone who says my son killed himself because he could not have sexual relations or intimacy with another human being is being intellectually dishonest.

Years ago, after I had recently married my husband, I was invited to a private gay party. As I engaged in conversation with some of the people there I started to feel nutty and astute. I claimed to be in love with my brother, and that we were planning to live together as sexual partners. They were stunned! "Why?" they asked. I used the very words that the homosexual agenda uses in their attempt to change our minds, our views, and our society.

I continued the conversation saying how we cannot choose who we love. I asked them why someone should pass judgment on us if we're different, consenting adults and are not causing anyone harm. I explained in detail that we would not have children due to the potential of the genetic consequences of the baby, but that we would love to adopt.

All of them were supportive of my make believe proposal without a single opponent. How could they have not? They could not form an objection as it would have been counterintuitive to their positions.

One of the most difficult things for me to swallow is the mantra of the LGBT community which says, "Be true to yourself." This mantra has become nothing more than a cliché, only applicable to those who will embrace the LGBT lifestyle. Anyone who dares to be "narrow-minded" enough to oppose it by "being true to themselves" and their own convictions will do so at their own peril. I assure you, the same tolerance, justice, fairness or equality that is demanded of you will not be given in return.

God's design is for a man and a woman to join together and not for a man or a woman to reject that which is natural for that which is unnatural. Neither a man with a man nor a woman with a woman is acceptable and is severely rebuked by God due to the purpose and plan He has intended for humanity. The Bible says:

> "You shall not lie with a male as with a woman. It *is* an abomination. Nor shall you mate with any animal, to defile yourself with it. Nor shall any woman stand before an animal to mate with it. It *is* perversion" (Leviticus 18:22-23 NKJV).

"If a man lies with a male as he lies with a woman, both of them have committed an abomination..." (Leviticus 20:13 NKJV).

"Because of this, God gave them over to shameful lusts. Even their women exchanged natural sexual relations for unnatural ones. In the same way, the men also abandoned natural relations with women and were inflamed with lust for one another. Men committed shameful acts with other men and received in themselves the due penalty for their error. Furthermore, just as they did not think it worthwhile to retain the knowledge of God, so God gave them over to a depraved mind, so that they do what ought not to be done" (Romans 1:26-28 NIV).

"Do you not know that the unrighteous will not inherit the kingdom of God? Do not be deceived. Neither fornicators, nor idolaters, nor adulterers, nor homosexuals, nor sodomites, nor thieves, nor covetous, nor drunkards, nor revilers, nor extortioners will inherit the kingdom of God" (1 Corinthians 6:9-10 NKJV).

Contrary to what many argue, they are not "born that way." We all have desires that are contrary to God's Word, but it doesn't mean that we act on them and live a lifestyle according to those desires. Tragically, Christians are embracing an idea of "political correctness," as secular humanists attempt to depict us who accept Scripture as ultimate truth as intolerant, and hateful. At this point, perhaps you perceive me as a hater—one who doesn't like people in the LGBT community. Let me make myself clear. I love the people in the LGBT community though not the agenda they are insisting we accept.

I am speaking as one who knows the inside. I had unfettered access, through my son, to the inner workings of this community. Still today, I keep close to a few of his friends who share with me the reality inside the doors of this culture.

I am a sinner and "mess" myself. However, I have no choice but to believe and to obey God's Word to the best of my ability. Though I sin and I do not excuse my sin, I also recognize that it is sin. I wake up every morning to the newness life and His mercy and grace. If my salvation resulted from my works (own ability), how could I be saved?

My heart is to follow the example of Jesus Christ, my hope of glory, who was obedient unto death. He died for me:

"And being found in appearance as a man, He humbled Himself and became obedient to the point of death, even the death of the cross" (Philippians 2:8 NKJV).

For this reason I come to you through these pages repeating Paul's words:

"But God forbid that I should boast except in the cross of our Lord Jesus Christ, by whom the world has been crucified to me, and I to the world" (Galatians 6:14 NKJV).

Let me put it this way; my son said he was homosexual, which makes me care a lot and have a pure heart for those in the lifestyle, but not for the lie behind the veil. I find no pleasure in hurting anyone, regardless of who they are, or what conditions they endure. I am one who embraces and does not reject. I rejoice when I see a soul mended and not destroyed. I am the type that will give all I can to make someone feel respected and loved, never harmed or outcast. Those who know me well would assure you that I care too much to hurt a person intentionally.

I will never advocate that the Church exercise a haughty spirit of judgment against anyone. Instead, the Lord commands us to a life of holiness. We must remember that, as Christians, we are all sinners saved by grace through faith in Jesus Christ. We were all on the wrong path, destined for hell aside from the saving knowledge of Jesus Christ, and His unmerited favor toward us. We are not less guilty of sin than those who practice the lifestyle of homosexuality. We are all at a crossroads!

I am pleased to recommend several books written by Joe Dallas—*"The Gay Gospel", "Desires in Conflict", "The Game Plan", "When Homosexuality Hits Home" and "The Complete Christian Guide to Understanding Homosexuality."* For many years, Joe Dallas was openly homosexual, extremely involved with the homosexual movement and attended a Christian church. He left the lifestyle, and firmly believes that change is possible and available. He is one of many who have left this lifestyle; proving that nothing is impossible for those who desire to leave it and reconcile with God through Jesus Christ.

Another book that I strongly recommend reading—*"Can You Be Gay and Christian: Responding with Truth & Love to Questions about Homosexuality"* by Dr. Michael L. Brown. Dr. Brown is a Jewish believer in Jesus (never in homosexual lifestyle) answers some timely and fundamental questions including whether you can really follow Jesus and practice homosexuality at the same time.

Hear What the Spirit is Saying

"I know your [record of] works and what you are doing; you are neither cold nor hot. Would that you were cold or hot! So, because you are lukewarm and neither cold nor hot, I will spew you out of My mouth...Behold, I stand at the door and knock; if anyone hears and listens to and heeds My voice and opens the door, I will come in to him and will eat with him, and he [will eat] with Me. He who overcomes (is victorious), I will grant him to sit beside Me on My throne, as I Myself overcame (was victorious) and sat down beside My Father on His throne. He who is able to hear, let him listen to and heed what the [Holy] Spirit says to the assemblies (churches)" (Revelation 3:15-22 AMP).

Jesus knows our works and He knows what we are doing. He said He would prefer us to be either hot or cold because if we are lukewarm He will spew us out of His mouth. A lukewarm Christian and church is one who compromises. For too long we have talked a good game while sitting on the sidelines yet doing nothing. Jesus wants us to care about the things that He cares about and love the things He loves. We cannot compromise any longer.

It is time for the church to be courageous and stand for truth or be forced into silence permanently. We have reached a tipping point in culture where if you don't embrace a certain agenda or dare to disagree then you will be silenced. You will be silenced by being vilified, marginalized, threatened, shamed, intimidated, mocked and branded as being oppressive. My question is, who's oppressing who?

The time has come that we stand for the truth of God's Word with power, clarity, conviction, and LOVE—

"For I am not ashamed of the gospel of Christ, for it is the power of God to salvation for everyone who believes..." (Romans 1:16 NKJV).

My Journey Continues

At the end of 2010 and the beginning of 2011, by God's grace, we were able to speak much into Jorge's life. During this time, we never stopped sharing the truth of salvation in Jesus Christ to dismantle the lies of Satan.

I never compromised the truth because I knew that the eternal destiny of my son was at stake. Near the end of his life, Jorge started to listen more to the words we spoke to him; my words, my mother's words, and the words of my husband. My mother and I agreed it was time for intense spiritual warfare. She prayed fervently that God would create opportunities where Jorge would have a personal and powerful encounter with Him. Salvation was important due to Jorge's life of habitual sin. I say habitual, even though we all sin, we who are in Christ do not live to sin; we might fall into sin on occasion. But sin is not the nature of our lives. However, when we sin, we must get up, repent, and receive God's forgiveness. God is faithful to forgive us as we continue walking the walk of faith. (1 John 1:9)

As I have said, Jorge's salvation was our primary goal in our praying. Scripture says in Mark 8:36, "What does it profit a man to gain the world but lose his soul?" It didn't matter how or when. We drew the line in the spiritual sand and refused to accept Jorge's fate of eternal damnation and separation from God. I am not referring to homosexuality alone, but a lifestyle of lying, deception, alcohol, addictions, and a life of brokenness bounded in self-idolatry. We serve a covenant-keeping God. We held onto Acts 16:31, where God promises: "Believe on the Lord Jesus Christ and you and your household will be saved." My main anguish wasn't that Jorge was gay, my primary concern was that Jorge was lost and needed to be born again.

Clearly, Jorge needed to come down from where he was to a place of repentance and live a clean, normal and honest working life. If Jorge had achieved all his dreams through commitment, integrity, and hard work my concerns would have diminished greatly. I would supported his positive efforts. Even then, if he continued the gay lifestyle, I would have kept speaking the truth according to biblical principles. I knew that sooner or later he would have to face his Creator, and give account and face the consequences, as we all will.

During this same time, Jorge had an epiphany. Following the suicide of one of his closest and dearest friends, I gave him Mary K. Baxter's popular book entitled, *A Divine Revelation of Hell*. I did this because I sensed Jorge was growing weary in his path and was ready to change the way he was living. I knew that dramatic change was coming, and I was afraid of this change. I needed assurance that he would awaken to the true reality of eternal life, and the consequences of a life lived outside of the boundaries that the Lord Jesus Christ has established for us.

Perhaps you are familiar with the principle from Ephesians 2:8-9, that we are not saved by our works, however, true faith in Christ Jesus will produce obedience to Him. Faith without works is similar to being loved without ever being hugged or kissed. We cannot dismiss works because faith without works of obedience is a dead faith. Our obedience is the manifestation of our faith. This is how we work out our salvation and perfect our sanctification. (Philippians 2:12)

One night Jorge called us devastated. He was crying uncontrollably. He told us that he didn't want to spend eternity outside of Jesus Christ and that he had been making the wrong choices for his eternal destiny. Again, this was not only about his homosexuality. Instead, this was about his life, in general, living outside the Lord's will and Grace. He recognized his self-centeredness and completely rebellious lifestyle against God's ways, specifically regarding the condition of his heart.

In February of 2011, things began to unravel completely as nearly all of his "friends," except a few, had eventually abandoned him while simultaneously stealing money, and valuables from his home. They left him alone in the worst moment of his life. He had depleted his financial resources and was experiencing debilitating depression and physical pain. Shortly after he stopped taking Hydrocodone he accidently cut off the tip of his finger off which caused excruciating pain. Due to his previous addiction, he explicitly told the hand surgeon not to provide him a prescription for Hydrocodone. He was written a prescription for another painkiller however due to the high dosage of Hydrocodone he had been taking for such a long period; nothing worked. His body craved the Hydrocodone more desperately than ever.

The loss of his "friends," when he needed them most; and no longer being able to provide the lifestyle to which they had become accustomed, brought him to a stark sense of reality. These "friends" for whom he had essentially rejected his only true family, for so many years; to live this crazy and unreasonable life, had left him alone and abandoned. Like rats rapidly escaping a sinking ship, they grabbed all they could carry on their way out.

I could see how agonizing this was for him to realize he was completely alone; except for his true family who had not abandoned him. It was at precisely this moment we had the miraculous opportunity to speak life into his languishing soul. Another reason this was a difficult time for Jorge was because he did not know how to live alone, or be by himself. For the first time in more than eight years, he wasn't surrounded by people who would validate all of his habits. One of the most insistent, effectual prayers that my mother and I were praying for him was that he would be forced to encounter who he had become, and who he could become in Jesus Christ! Jorge needed to be alone, without all the truth-defying distractions so he could get close enough to the Lord to hear His voice. Though he was confused, Jorge needed to find himself face to face with the Lord and be in a position where his only answer was God! It would be in this environment that he would be forced to make a life-changing decision!

During the last weeks of his life, Jorge tried to surround himself with "good things," including several Bibles. He was desperate to find the Lord, and to find peace in the midst of the greatest storm of his life. He even created a "prayer room" in his house, and told me that it was the place where he would go to seek God. Jorge was trying so hard to find the way back. It was obvious to us that though he was still confused, he no longer wanted to live the lifestyle he had lived for so long. He had finally realized that lifestyle was a lie, and it had robbed him of so much, including knowing who he really was. Jorge was very broken and emotionally damaged. He made his prayer room because he knew that I had one in my house. He told me, "I bow on my knees everyday mama, and asked God to forgive me for the wrong I have done, for the pain I have caused others and to myself, mama." He also began to call everyone he knew to tell them that he loved them, and to ask for their forgiveness if he had done anything wrong to them. I only found this out later. Jorge was awake and desperate to find his way back.

Jorge had so many beautiful characteristics, and one of his best was that he was noble. Amazingly, he never allowed himself to store resentment or unforgiveness in his heart. No matter what anyone did to him, somehow he would always forgive. This is not to say that he did not do wrong to others.

But overall, his heart remained that of a child seeking love, mercy, compassion, and family.

During the lowest point of Jorge's path, after his so-called friends abandoned him, he disclosed to my husband that he had an addiction to Hydrocodone. He disclosed this the week after my surgery in his office. He said that a doctor had told him that he was going to die due to his addiction. He told George that he didn't want to die, or to be destroyed by his addiction and as a result he was committed to overcoming it.

Jorge's addiction to Hydrocodone began after having several surgeries in 2010. These surgeries caused a high degree of pain, but one thing Jorge quickly discovered was the pain killing effects and the by-product was the euphoria the opiates could cause in higher dosages. Quickly the dosages increased with the refills coming as quickly as requested leading to addiction over nine months. He would take as many as 26 pills per day, which left him almost incapacitated. Jorge was depressed. He felt his life was coming to an end, and he felt at a loss for answers and overtaken by regret. The medication gave him the euphoria he needed to have a little bit of optimism in his life and hope for his future. Jorge's nervous system had been contaminated and compromised.

When a person lives a life that he knows in his heart of hearts is wrong, he looks for ways to numb the pain. Jorge needed the pills to survive each day. However, he didn't understand that he wasn't going to be able to stop "cold turkey" which he did. Opiates are similar to cocaine, which he had done before and also stopped "cold turkey." After Jorge's death, we were told by separate doctors that he needed to be under the care of specialists to properly customize and even supervise a treatment program. A program designed to help him "step down" off of the opiates to minimize withdrawal effects on his central nervous system and body. Opiates can rewire your brain which is why they are so addictive. How deadly is ignorance? What a great price for us to pay for it. No wonder the Lord says that His people are destroyed for lack of knowledge. We often think, if only we had known.

Instead, Jorge just stopped taking the opiates. As a consequence, he completely lost his grasp of reality and became delusional. Shortly after midnight on March 9th, 2011, my son stepped into his walk-in closet, took a gun, placed it to his head and pulled the trigger. He died instantly. Was it the opiates? Was it the identity crisis? Was it both? Only God knows.

It is not because he is my son that I will say this, but my family and I have received numerous confirmations that the Lord Jesus Christ allowed my son to enter His Kingdom that night. He has been so kind to me to give me a vision of the moment my dear Jorge entered Heaven. God was so gracious and gentle as He knew my knowledge of His Word and the basic foundations of His saving grace. He came to me one night around 3:00 a.m. and spoke directly to my heart the confirming word that Jorge had entered His Kingdom. He clearly articulated why Jorge was allowed to enter into the

Lord's rest. Please always remember that only the Lord knows the last cry of a person's heart. Making it imperative for us to lovingly minister the incorruptible Word of God to our lost loved ones; despite their resistance and without questioning the impact. God knows.

Once again, please let me stress that I am not saying, nor am I implying in any way that suicide is okay. To the contrary, I am not condoning suicide or suggesting that God considers it a minor infraction. I am not saying that God can or will simply overlook it. Absolutely not! It is the worst decision a person can make. It is the biggest risk one can take affecting the destiny of their eternal spirit, not to mention the devastating impact it has on the lives of those touched by it. I cannot begin to describe the pain, suffering and the complete devastation it brings to the loved ones left behind. Every situation is unique, and I would venture to say that in most cases if a person commits this horrific and violent act, they can end up on the wrong side of eternity. It is a cowardly and selfish decision that is never God's will. We are to live and not die! The Bible tells us in Philippians 4:19 tells us that, "the Lord will provide for all of our needs according to His riches in glory by Christ Jesus."

The Lord can and will heal! The Lord can and will restore! The Lord offers each of us new life in Him, and the Lord makes a way where there seems to be no way. We must trust in the Lord and in the power of His might to save us, and to establish us with new life in Him.

Coming Back (The Last Year)

The Book of Ephesians tells us —

> "Now to Him Who, by (in consequence of) the [action of His] power that is at work within us, is able to [carry out His purpose and] do superabundantly, far over *and* above all that we [dare] ask or think [infinitely beyond our highest prayers, desires, thoughts, hopes, or dreams]" (Eph 3:20 AMP).

I leave you with this Scripture written by the Apostle Paul during a time of great affliction —

> "However, we possess this precious treasure [the divine Light of the Gospel] in [frail, human] vessels of earth, that the grandeur *and* exceeding greatness of the power may be shown to be from God and not from ourselves. We are hedged in (pressed) on every side [troubled and oppressed in every way], but not cramped *or* crushed; we suffer embarrassments *and* are perplexed *and* unable to find a way out, but not driven to despair; We are pursued (persecuted and hard driven), but not deserted [to stand alone]; we are struck down to the ground, but never struck out *and* destroyed" (2 Corinthians 4:7-9 AMP).

My Son Killed Himself

Chapter Six
MY STAND

"Many families become damaged, debased or entirely destroyed when they encounter the monster of addiction in their midst. Often blindsided by their love for the one in imminent danger, they vehemently try to stop the departure and the certain destruction as they fervently attempt to become the rescuers. Most are completely unprepared and unaware how to save their loved one from this damaging habit.

Not being aware that they have opened the doors of the house to the wings of furious storms, unstoppable flows of tsunamis, unquenchable fire that will put every person in the house in jeopardy, leaving everybody aboard to ride the daily roller coaster of this destructive practice."

-Dr. Red, Psychotherapist, and
Marriage and Family Expert

Most of us are familiar when Jesus spoke of the parable of The Prodigal Son. Before I discuss the importance of my position and the motivation behind it, let's review the parable of Jesus from the Book of Luke (15:11-32):

"And He said, There was a certain man who had two sons; And the younger of them said to his father, Father, give me the part of the property that falls [to me]. And he divided the estate between them. And not many days after that, the younger son gathered up all that he had and journeyed into a distant country, and there he wasted his fortune in reckless and loose [from restraint] living. And when he had spent all he had, a mighty famine came upon that country, and he began to fall behind and be in want. So he went and forced (glued) himself upon one of the citizens of that country, who sent him into his fields to feed hogs. And he would gladly have fed on and filled his belly with the carob pods that the hogs were eating, but [they could not satisfy his hunger and] nobody gave him anything [better]. Then when he came to himself, he said, How many hired servants of my father have enough food, and [even food] to spare, but I am perishing (dying) here of hunger! I will get up and go to my father, and I will say to him, Father, I have sinned against heaven and in your sight. I am no longer worthy to be called your son; [just] make me like one of your hired servants. So he got up and came to his [own] father. But while he was still a long way off, his father saw him and was moved with pity and tenderness [for him]; and he ran and embraced him and kissed him [fervently]. And the son said to him, Father, I have sinned against heaven and in your sight; I am no longer worthy to be called your son [I no longer deserve to be recognized as a son of yours]! But the father said to his bond servants bring quickly the best robe (the festive robe of honor) and put it on him; and give him a ring for his hand and sandals for his feet. And bring out that [wheat-] fattened calf and kill it; and let us revel and feast and be happy and make merry, Because this my son was dead and is alive again; he was lost and is found! And they began to revel and feast and make merry. But his older son was in the field; and as he returned and came near the house, he heard music and dancing. And having called one of the servant [boys] to him, he began to ask what this meant. And he said to him, your brother has come, and your father has killed that [wheat-] fattened calf, because he has received him back safe and well. But [the elder brother] was angry [with deep-seated wrath] and resolved not to go in. Then his father came out and began to plead with him, but he answered his father, Look! These many years I have served you, and I have never disobeyed your command. Yet you never gave me [so much as] a [little] kid, that I might revel and feast and be happy and make merry with my friends; But when this son of yours arrived, who has devoured your estate with immoral women; you have killed for him that [wheat-] fattened calf! And the father said to him, Son, you are always with me, and all that is mine is yours. But it was fitting to make merry, to revel and feast and rejoice, for this brother of yours was dead and is alive again! He was lost and is found" (Luke 15:11-32 AMP).

One of the areas that shocked me the most about this story was the reaction of the father. Not only did he allow the son to leave without restraint, but he also gave the son what he requested; perhaps deeply hoping for his son's future success. As a mother, I am well aware that each of us, as parents, (unless we are in full denial) is capable of recognizing our children's character and temperament. This father was probably aware of his son's lack of common sense, and the terrible consequences that the son's decision would likely bring.

Equally surprising was that the father never followed him. He didn't even send money to help him when he encountered calamity. He didn't beg his son to return. He obviously didn't feel responsible or guilty for his son's decision. In addition to that, he didn't allow himself to become his son's enabler.

I understand the pain, loss, guilt, and desperation the loss of a child brings. Too many parents of wayward children believe the only way they could have entered this darkness is because we have let them down in one way or another. In doing so, we allow false guilt and condemnation to overtake us. Many factors can come into play which are neither easy nor simple.

It is extremely difficult to watch a son or daughter choose a terrible path. As parents or friends, we rely on pure love, hoping we can save them. We determine that we will somehow cause them come to their senses, and convince them with sound logic to stop living a destructive lifestyle. I wish this were true, unfortunately, most of the time it is not. Believe me when I say I know from experience how hard this is!

In fact, Dr. Red once told me—

"The longer we live in this terrible nightmare, the more we start giving up. We lose our hope, our strength, and finally reach a point we are ready to accept the final outcome, even if it is death. We are ready for it because we are losing our own lives, in our intent to rescue them. After a while, we simply want the pain to end and to have some peace and rest."

He also told me—

"When we allow the boundaries of conduct to be broken in our household, especially with addictions, we have done two things: we have accepted the corruption of the household, and we have made the recovery of the person with the issue to linger longer and potentially impossible to overcome. They exert control over our lives, and we are relegated to accept the pain as captives of this increasingly unfamiliar person."

Dr. Red held a firm conviction that the treatment of most people with addictions became a financially lucrative business with a very low success ratio for the person being treated. His belief was once a member of the household had broken the boundaries of trust and disrespect they opened doors that posed a great danger to the household. These open doors threatened to overtake each member of the household making it necessary to impose harsh and tough decisions to protect the rest of the family. He was confident that this made it a crucial time to send a clear and strong message of tough love. In our conversations part of the application of tough love regarding teens using drugs and alcohol were—

"As soon an addiction trend is discovered by the parents; they must go and interrogate friends, family members, school officials or anyone else their child meets frequently.

The rules are simple. The teen is commanded by the parents to abstain, and to seek counseling to help them regain control over their lives. If this fails, the parents will find a counseling/treatment center to which they can send the rebellious teen to live for a while. If the teen leaves the premises of that place, is uncooperative, and does not comply with and live under their regulations, he or she will be on their own until they comply with the parents' rules."

I can assure you that every step we took as a family concerning my son's recovery was handled this way. Many of the decisions we made were a carbon copy of the tough love philosophy, which also follows the biblical example of the prodigal son. The Word of God teaches us to honor our fathers and mothers. This is one of the core commandments of the Lord, we find in Exodus 20:12. It brings a promise of a long, healthy and prosperous life. Respect is central to Jesus' and the apostle's teaching. It is the foundation of true love.

Disrespect is a key characteristic of a rebellious spirit which challenges God, parents, and society.

As the family journeyed more deeply into this terrible storm, I can see how blessed we were to receive guidance from Dr. Red, and from our mentor and spiritual father, Pastor Dr. John R. Counts. We depended so much on his guidance. My husband, George found himself in the most conflicted position as a new leader and a member of our household. It was terrible for him, seeing the events get progressively worse. He had no choice but to stand tall and strong at times against, Jorge, my first born. I was growing spiritually, as a woman of God, and I knew my emotions were going to be very deceptive. I learned to depend on my husband's godly wisdom, the advice of Dr. Red, and my spiritual parents' mentoring.

At times, it was difficult for me to rely on the advice of others, especially when I knew they couldn't love my son as much as I did. But, I was wise enough to understand that my thinking wasn't objective in the midst of the conflict we were experiencing. I had to rely on God, on the advice of a skilled expert like Dr. Red, on a strong husband, and the support of Pastor Counts. In a sense, my other son and I were being protected by these wonderful people from our flesh and blood. I had the common sense to allow these people to guide me through this valley of darkness, and to shelter my second son. Remember, he was only seven years old when all of this started. We wanted to make sure that Jorge's terrible decisions and behavior would not negatively affect his brother.

It was hard through the years for us not to allow him to spend time with his brother. Here and there Jorge would pass by, visit me, or I would meet him somewhere. As hard as it was for me as a mother I knew it was in the best interest of his younger brother to keep as much distance as possible. There was too much risk of him leaving an imprint on his impressionable mind and heart. As heartbreaking as it was, due to Jorge's decisions and condition, many Holiday's including Christmas, Thanksgiving, Mother's Day's, and birthday celebrations were spent without him.

Dr. Red prepared me for the moment when Jorge was going to call hungry, and ask me for food. He told me that when he called asking me for even a hamburger, I was not to give in. He said, "The sooner he (Jorge) realizes the consequences of his terrible decisions and hits bottom, the sooner his possible recovery can be." I said, "His possible recovery?" He said, "Yes because each person has their own bottom, and for some, the bottom is death."

Sure enough, the day came when Jorge called and asked me to order and pay for a pizza for him because he was hungry. I had prayed that day would never come, and I remember it as it though it was yesterday. I said, "No son, sorry. You chose the life you are living." I recall hanging up the phone and hearing him scream, "I hate you... I hate you!" I sobbed as never before. I knew he must hit bottom at all cost for his sake.

I am not going to tell you whether this system worked or not for our family. After all, it's a personal decision a person like Jorge must make to recover from a life on the brink of hell. One way to possibly assess the progress of a person in that situation who begins listening to those who are ministering life and hope to them is if they begin making steps to meet halfway. I strongly believe that we are what we desire and choose to be in this life, without excuses. I have seen, and I have read many books about people who emerged victorious from the most inhospitable environments and abusive homes. I have been inspired to read the stories of how they made the decision to rise above their circumstances and succeed. I also understand that, for most people, this is extremely hard and requires a tough person with a clear vision of the future they desire. That determination comes from within an individual.

One time while visiting with Dr. Red, he explained to me that the vast majority of people who seek counseling don't desire to change. Most people seek counseling to complain, to talk about their issues, to release the pressure and go back to the same life.

My wise husband says, "Do not give advice unless asked. Even then have the wisdom to understand that most people don't want to hear the truth, all they want is people to listen. Rarely will they do anything with what you tell them."

The real obstacle to a healthy and successful recovery and control of a person's life is self-pity. As Dr. Red expressed, "Most people love to hold tight to the blanket of self-indulgent defeatism and pity parties because they like to maintain control of their position as a victim."

To change, a person has to let go of the blame, the irresponsibility, and accept accountability on their part. They must be ready to see inside themselves, and meditate upon their actions and reactions. If they are to move forward to a new beginning, they need to be brave enough to look in the mirror and see who they really are. They need to be willing to move forward without needing to know "the whys," or to place blame, or even completely understand their deficiencies and internal conflicts.

I strongly believe that the hardest thing for a human to do is to "self-see;" to look inside and admit our own shortcomings. We need to take ownership of the findings and take actions necessary to correct them.

This is why we find so many good-hearted and well-intended Christians living mediocre lives, broken and bitter, due to multiple levels of resentment. They lack joy, are dissatisfied, disillusioned, defeated, and depressed. Some are addicted, walking according to the world's system, conflicted between the flesh and the spirit, void of Godly character, and victims of their circumstances. The reason does not necessarily rest in their doctrine, or in the examples provided by Jesus' life and the lives of the saints. It rests with them. We are the ones whose role it is to follow the Word of God when it says, "Do not be conformed to the World but renew your mind with the Word of God" (Romans 12:1-2). Take action!

Back to Jorge

Even after Jorge returned from abusing drugs, I strongly held my position concerning family interaction. I needed to because Jorge was very smart, cunning and astute. My son knew that I adored him, but limits and boundaries were a must with Jorge. Besides, I couldn't change the rules out of fear, or out of my love for him. I could not afford to give into his bratty tantrums or ideas, even if it meant losing a relationship with him again. He knew I loved him. I needed to send Him a clear and unmistakable message for the rest of his life on earth and beyond! He needed to think about where he was going to spend eternity.

My mother and I prayed many times to the Father in Heaven that He would bring Jorge to his knees; to create a moment where he would experience a face to face encounter with God. After many years of praying, we determined that if Jorge were so stubborn that if only through death he would see the truth, then we would have to accept this. We knew that if he didn't see the truth of Jesus Christ, he would be lost forever. We never compromised because his destiny was at stake, and we were going to do everything possible to prevent his tragic ending outside God's goodness and benefits for eternity. Remember, there is no goodness outside of God's realm. True goodness and love exist only within His kingdom.

Remember, for us Christians, this life, and its glories cannot compare to eternity and the life that we will spend with God. Eternal resurrection is the center of our faith and our lives. For us, we know that the ultimate prize is to enter the Kingdom of God and spend all of eternity under His lordship and in His custody. Things that we do on earth have the potential of detouring us and bringing us to the wrong destination. As I've said previously, it's not that salvation is by works, because it is not. Salvation is by God's grace through faith in Him. As the Bible declares in Ephesians 2:8, "we are saved by grace through faith and not by works lest any man should brag." It is one that trusts in, adheres to and relies on the work of Jesus on the cross and His resurrection as recorded in God's Word. Without this solid foundation, our faith is false.

"For no other foundation can anyone lay than that which is [already] laid, which is Jesus Christ (the Messiah, the Anointed One)" (1 Corinthians 3:11 AMP).

Faith Triumphs in the Midst of Trouble

"Therefore, having been justified by faith, we have peace with God through our Lord Jesus Christ, through whom also we have access by faith into this grace in which we stand, and rejoice in hope of the glory of God. And not only that, but we also glory in tribulations, knowing that tribulation produces perseverance; and perseverance, character; and character, hope" (Romans 5:1-4 NKJV).

Many parents do their best to accommodate their children's ways and what they accept as the truth concerning their faith. Many times they change their views for fear that they will jeopardize their relationship with their sons or daughters. But in the end, if we accept anything that is not of God, we will be open to accepting everything that is not of God. It will absolutely jeopardize the potential of their eternal Salvation.

Christ's story of the prodigal son is a great story, with an amazing ending. It demonstrates the result of not compromising or caving in to pressure from, or the blaming of our children. The prodigal after being out of his parent's home for apparently many years made a decision to return even if he had to suffer the indignity of being a family servant. Finally after receiving the fruit of his unmanageable and defiant character he determined it was much better to be a servant in his father's house than continue his rebellious life which had brought him nothing of value. He had lost his name's meaning, his identity, his sense of worth and found himself in a hog pen, eating with hogs. It was there that he eventually lost his pride. He had to gain knowledge, wisdom, and understanding. You see, when a person refuses to learn proper values in their parents' homes, they will learn the world's values on the streets. Life teaches lessons you will never forget.

On a joyful note, upon his return to his father's house, the prodigal found (perhaps for the first time in his life) an unpretentious meek heart and a humble spirit. The following verses illustrate the change that took place in his heart:

"Rebellion is as sinful as witchcraft and stubbornness as bad as worshiping idols" (1 Samuel 15:23 NIV).

"If my people who are called by my name, will humble themselves and pray and seek my face and turn from their wicked ways, I will hear from Heaven and will forgive their sins and restore their land" (2 Chronicles 7:14 NLT).

"And whoever exalts himself will be humbled, and he who humbles himself will be exalted" (Matthew 23:2 NKJV).

If you, (mom or dad, brother or sister, relative or friend) feel as if you are in the process of losing your loved one, I pray that our Lord in Heaven will help you, guide you, and encourage your faith. I pray that you maintain your strength as you stand in the gap for your lost loved one. Remember, you cannot do this alone. You need a support system that will empower and direct you. You need people to rely and depend upon for spiritual and emotional inspiration. To a large extent, they will be your true eyes and ears to help you recognize manipulation. Many times your loved one will manipulate you to use you to get what he or she needs *at* the moment which will leave you feeling defrauded.

Chapter Seven
SIN

The Wages of Sin

"For the wages which sin pays is death, but the [bountiful] free gift of God is eternal life through (in union with) Jesus Christ our Lord" (Romans 6:23 AMP).

"There is a way which seems right to a man and appears straight before him, but at the end of it is the way of death" (Proverbs 14:12 AMP).

What is sin? In the simplest way I can define it, sin is any action contrary to God's laws, or His character, nature, constitution, temperament and representation, image, or likeness. Sin is any heart attitude that challenges His Sovereignty and opposes Him. Sin is anything that separates us from God.

How Does Sin Work?

"Let no one say when he is tempted, 'I am tempted by God'; for God cannot be tempted by evil, nor does He Himself tempt anyone. But each one is tempted when he is drawn away by his own desires and enticed. Then, when desire has conceived, it gives birth to sin; and sin, when it is full-grown, brings forth death" (James 1:13-15 NKJV).

In other words, a person is tempted by his or her own desires or cravings. Temptation can only be resisted with the power of God's Holy Spirit requiring that you be born again (Jesus Christ living on the inside of you). The Book of James writes, "Submit to God, resist the devil and he will flee from you" (James 4:7).

It is vital for us to understand that if we operate in the Lord's power, we have the strength to resist sinful, errant, immoral, and wicked behavior. We need to submit our desires, physical wants and passions to God, including our earthly nature. However, if we allow ourselves to dwell on the sinful desire, sin will be conceived in our minds, and be expressed by our behavior. After this, our sinful desires become stronger and justifiable in our minds.

If a true conviction of wrongdoing doesn't sink in, the particular sin or sins will grow even stronger and become established in our patterns of thinking and living. Then they will expand into different areas of our soul (will, mind and emotions). The consequences of sin are an uneasy feeling of being in disharmony with God. For example, when we fight with our loved ones, we are not in one accord with Him. Continual sinful living produces death.

"Examine and test and evaluate your own selves to see whether you are holding to your faith and showing the proper fruits of it..." (2 Corinthians 13:5 AMP).

With great sadness, looking back I clearly recall when and how my son started down the path of sin, and how his sins began to multiply and entangle him more and more. I gradually watched my lovely son abandon himself and the principles I taught him for a life of immorality and self-indulgence. I had never seen first-hand how polluted a life can become when the conscience becomes so darkened, and the lines of right and wrong become blurred. A blindness of the soul sets in. Sin begins to sound desirable and pleasing to the flesh, but sin will eventually tear you down, minimize your worth, and destroy your life. We need to guard our souls and be cautious of those with whom we choose to associate. Scripture teaches, "Do not be misled: Bad company corrupts good character..." (1 Corinthians 15:33).

We all sin because we have been born with a sinful nature that we inherited from Adam. Without repentance, we will certainly receive the reward (consequences) of our sin when we abide (live a lifestyle of) in sin. We cannot dwell on sinful acts, allow sin to rule our conscience, rebel against God, and stop believing and obeying His Word. We are saved by faith, but faith is a verb that requires action. The evidence of our faith in God's Word is our obedience to His will. We will not act upon that which we don't believe in (trust in, adhere to, rely upon).

Faith believes (trust in, adhere to, rely upon) God's Word. How long could it take for a person dwelling and living a lifestyle of sin to annul his faith? Only God knows. But, we cannot afford to believe that it is not possible. Jesus said:

> "You have a few names even in Sardis, who have not defiled their garments; and they shall walk with Me in white, for they are worthy. He who overcomes shall be clothed in white garments, and I will not blot out his name from the Book of Life; but I will confess his name before My Father and before His angels" (Revelation 3:4-5 NKJV).

Is it faith by works? Absolutely not, however, the Bible is clear. Read Jesus's words, "But why do you call Me 'Lord, Lord,' and not do the things which I say" (Luke 6:46 NKJV)?

The Bible tells us that faith without works is dead. We must understand that it is not about us but all about Him. The reason our faith produces works is because it is not based on us or our own ability or our own strength. Instead, our faith produces works when we allow the Holy Spirit, who is Christ in Us the Hope of Glory to do the work within us. Then the work of the Holy Spirit in us will produce the works/fruits that make our faith alive, not dead. I say it again, it is not about us, but it is all about Him! It is His Word that transform and bring life as we are His mouthpiece to the world.

> "I have come as a light into the world, whoever believes in Me should not abide in darkness. And if anyone hears My words and does not believe, I do not judge him; for I did not come to judge the world but to save the world. He who rejects Me, and does not receive My words, has that which judge him — the word that I have spoken will judge him in the last day" (John 12:46-48 NKJV).

God strongly warns us about sin in the Old Testament, as well as in the New Testament. As we read from Book to Book through the Bible, we learn that the result of man's sin has turned history into a tragic drama that repeats itself time and time again with each successive generation. Due to the consequences of his sin, man has paid an exorbitant price on both a personal and a societal level.

We all have fallen into the sin of pride, blind to the truth, and to what is honorable, dignifying, worthy of grace and virtue. Our self-righteous egos have grown boastful, conceited, and narcissistic. As a society, we have become insolent, unruly, disoriented, and disobedient to parents. We are being consumed by our lust for power, position, and this world's riches. Many of our homes have become nothing more than battlefields for power and control.

In the Old Testament story of Lot, who lived in Sodom, God sent two angels to rescue him and his family. After being rescued by angels, Lot found himself in a cave with his two daughters. Assuming it was the end of civilization (of the world), they plotted to make their father drunk, to have sex with him and have children. Not only did they conceive the plot, but they carried out their plan.

I always wonder how they could have conceived such thing. However, it is easier to understand after we read the story. Raised in a land that was morally corrupt their consciences were darkened by the society in which they lived. They were able to conceive such a thing because they were quite familiar with the ways of sin (moral decay).

How profoundly sad I was every time I dealt with my son's twisted moral principles (precepts, values, principles, and ethics). He had adopted the ways of sin, and, as a result, became increasingly blind to his sins. Having fun, and living for the moment was the norm. A self-destructive behavior became a way of life.

The nature of God within us cries out so painfully loud that I often think that we attempt to silence Him by saturating ourselves with temporary, external and nonsensical formulas for happiness. Without even realizing it our addictions, our insatiable desires to accumulate things that are just temporary and our quest for success are nothing more than our attempts to fill a void in our life. An attempt to fill the void left by an empty hole of pain, memories of abandonment, hurt and sorrow, a lack of identity or low self-worth. How can a person judge right from wrong when everyone around him/her practices a lifestyle of sin freely without conscience? The Bible warns us that the ways of sin are the ways of death.

"But how are people to call upon Him Whom they have not believed [in Whom they have no faith, on Whom they have no reliance]? And how are they to believe in Him [adhere to, trust in, and rely upon Him] of Whom they have never heard? And how are they to hear without a preacher" (Romans 10:14 AMP)?

God's Authentic and Unquenchable Love

THE STORY OF HOSEA

The book of Hosea in the Old Testament is one of my favorite books of the Bible. It demonstrates so vividly the way God loves us, sinners. The first time I read Hosea, I could hardly believe what I was reading. The omnipotent Creator God, the Great I AM, reveals Himself to us in the most tender and loving way. This God, who sits on the throne above, who reigns with power and might, allowed Himself to be vulnerable to the people He had chosen for Himself. I felt His love so real, so profound, and unmovable as I read Hosea's story.

The prophet Hosea wrote the book of Hosea around 750 B.C. About this time, the Lord called Hosea to marry a harlot (prostitute). Society during this time was not favorable to God. His people were in moral blindness. They had turned away from Him to fulfill their lustful desires. They enjoyed a relatively good life regarding peace and prosperity; however because the people had corrupted leaders, though prosperous, their time of abundance seemed threatened by anarchy. Even members of the priesthood were dishonest and were failing to provide righteous guidance for the people.

It was at a time like this that God called His prophet, Hosea, to undertake an extremely difficult task. Hosea had been consecrated to the Lord to hear his voice, to correct and to guide His people, was instructed by God to marry a woman of the night, a streetwalker, a prostitute. Could you have ever thought such an idea would have come from God? No way, we are too devout to consider such a thing. But God's plans and purposes are noble and perfect; His ways are not our ways, and in Him there is no darkness.

Of course, the Lord knew His unique plan from the moment Hosea was conceived in his mother's womb. When he was born, he was given the name Hosea, which means "deliverance" or "salvation." We can be sure that Hosea was ready for the task since he was in tune with God's heart, His concerns, and His love for His people. It would be a costly assignment for Hosea. For one, it would cost him his pride.

However, I suspect that as a true man of God, Hosea had consecrated his pride long before, considering what the people thought of him. True Prophets are never welcomed in times of societal idolatry and debauchery.

In spite of those conditions, God assigned Hosea to an extremely difficult mission that would communicate God's love, and the hope that awaits sinners who repent and return to Him. The Book of Hosea is about a people who needed to hear about God's steadfast, unchanging love; and about a God, who was willing to reveal it to them. At that time, love was perceived in a wrong way and carried with it wrong motives and agendas.

The people thought that love was something that could be purchased. It was viewed as something to be pursued for our own benefit, our own self-gratification, and that loving unworthy objects could bring positive results.

"For she said, 'I will go after my lovers, who give me my bread and my water, my wool and my linen, my oil and my drink'" (Hosea 2:5).

"Ephraim has hired lovers…" (Hosea 8:9).

"But they went to Baal Peor and separated themselves to that shame; they became an abomination like the thing they loved" (Hosea 9:10).

God wanted His people to recognize and value His infinite love for them, which reaches out to us unlikely, unworthy objects. (Romans 5:8) Hosea's story illustrates God's gentle hand of discipline, and His frustration seeing His people stray from Him again and again; constantly running and resisting His love.

A commentary in The New Spirit-Filled Life Bible says that these people were not inclined to listen and were not likely to have understood if they had listened. They were spiritually deaf, blind, and stubborn.

> "For rebellion is as the sin of witchcraft, and stubbornness is as idolatry and teraphim (household good luck images). Because you have rejected the word of the Lord, He also has rejected you from being king" (1 Samuel 15:23 AMP).

Hosea's mission was to love a harlot who insisted on having affairs with other men; and who would walk away from his loving arms to find pleasure in the arms of other men. Regardless of how much Hosea loved and treasured her, she would continue to go astray.

"Then said the Lord to me, Go again, love [the same] woman [Gomer] who is beloved of a paramour and is an adulteress, even as the Lord loves the children of Israel, though they turn to other gods and love cakes of raisins [used in the sacrificial feasts in idol worship]. So I bought her for fifteen pieces of silver and a homer and a half of barley [the price of a slave]" (Hosea 3:1-2 AMP).

Nevertheless, the Lord tells Hosea:

— Love her fully to the extent of conceiving children with her" (Hosea 1:3).

— Go after her and bring her back when she strays" (Hosea 3:1).

Through Hosea's obedience, God would show His profound and unquenchable love toward the ones who had walked away from His love and provision. This world is looking for authentic love, love that can only be found in the arms of a loving Savior. We are to be conduits of God's love, those who will love sinners while hating the sin. Sin defiles, defeats, and brings spiritual death and eternal separation from Him.

The church has always found it difficult to love and value "the sinner" who was created in the image of God while rejecting the sin nature. We seem to swing like pendulums, either getting close to sinners and joining with them in their sin, or completely casting them aside as if they are of no value to God. We tend to forget that Jesus came to seek and to save sinners.

It is amazing to me how faithfully our loving God strives to rescue and restore us to full honor and dignity. He is fully committed to bringing His creation, back to Himself at all costs. As necessary, He corrects, rebukes, chastises, and even leaves us to ourselves for a time until we conclude that He is the one who truly loves us, with an honest and sincere love. He does this, so we will humble ourselves, appreciate Him, and accept all He has for us. Below is the part of the Book of Hosea when God takes the vows of marriage with His people. In it, He expresses His pure love and devotion for us (His bride) who continue backsliding.

"And it shall be in that day, says the Lord, that you will call Me Ishi [my Husband], and you shall no more call Me Baali [my Baal]. For I will take away the names of Baalim [the Baals] out of her mouth, and they shall no more be mentioned *or* seriously remembered by their name. And in that day will I make a covenant for Israel…And I will betroth you to Me forever;

yes, I will betroth you to Me in righteousness and justice, in steadfast love, and in mercy.

"I will even betroth you to Me in stability *and* in faithfulness, and you shall know (recognize, be acquainted with, appreciate, give heed to, and cherish) the Lord" (Hosea 2:16-20 AMP).

It breaks my heart to realize how unworthy I am of Him; and yet how precious I am to Him.

Satan is incapable of understanding God's love, and salvation. Satan despises us because he despises God and that we have been created in God's image. He despises us because God loves us so much that He would leave His Kingdom in Heaven and come as a servant and die on the cross for us! What victory! On that cross, Satan thought he had the victory. Instead, it was Jesus' death, burial and resurrection on the third day that defeated Satan. Jesus became our Way (the only Way) to a personal relationship with God the Father.

Once buried in our own sin and incapable of entering Heaven now when we truly enter into a relationship with Jesus Christ everything changes. We are made righteous and Heaven-ready by the blood Jesus shed for us. We may now enter Heaven's gates with our heads held high as sons and daughters of the King.

I remember as though it were yesterday crying while driving to work one cloudy and rainy day. Suddenly, I sensed the Lord's voice saying—

> "Where there is brokenness, I restore it. When something is lost, I find it. Where there is only darkness and confusion, I bring light and clarity. Where there seems to be no 'way', I make a 'way.' When the world says, 'it's over;' I say 'it's just beginning.' When Satan says, 'this person is mine, destroyed and condemned;' I say, 'that one belongs to Me, I will restore and save them."

God's love toward us is so powerful which is why I am not ashamed of His Gospel or His Name. The great sorrow is that when we walk away from God's ways, we also walk away from Him and His protection. Truly, if we are His children, He will deal with us accordingly. Let's praise Him for disciplining, rebuking and chastising us as needed! (Hebrews 12:6) It is because he disciplines us that we know that He loves us and that He is our Daddy in Heaven! What father that loves his children doesn't discipline them?

It is a shame that many times our rebellious hearts take us into dangerous territories. On these occasions, we open the doors of our lives to darkness, which will destroy us spiritually and physically. Our minds and consciences

Sin

become darkened to God's truth. Our insubordinate, stubborn acts of sin bring God's discipline and allow us to reap what we have planted with our disobedience. At times, it will feel as though He's abandoned us—which He never will. The truth is we just don't like to be told the truth and we sure don't like to be disciplined.

In the Book of Hosea we read:

> "My people are destroyed for lack of knowledge. Because you have rejected knowledge, I also will reject you from being a priest for Me; Because you have forgotten the law of your God, I also will forget your children. The more they increased, The more they sinned against Me; I will change their glory into shame. They eat up the sin of My people; They set their heart on their iniquity. And it shall be: like people, like a priest. So I will punish them for their ways, And reward them for their deeds. For they shall eat, but not have enough; They shall commit harlotry, but not increase; Because they have ceased obeying the LORD" (Hosea 4:6-10 NKJV).

Reading the book of Hosea, we also find God's anger for the lack of shame His people have regarding the sinful condition of their hearts. We can be certain that He will deal

171

with us as He dealt with them. He will chastise us as He chastised them. God will allow us to suffer the consequences of our deserting His profitable ways, and we will receive the penalty just like they received for their disobedience.

I know that in today's culture it isn't popular to mention sin let alone the consequences of sin. Please understand that I've shared my son's story within the pages of this book to warn others; keeping in mind that I am also a sinner saved by grace. As a sinner (one that sins and not engages in a lifestyle of sin), I require God's grace that I can only receive because I have been saved, and He lives in me.

Grace is unmerited favor which means that there is nothing I can do in my own ability to earn my salvation. Nothing I can do is sufficient. It is only by the work of Jesus Christ through His death, burial and resurrection and by His presence living in me. If it were not so then I would be living according to my own ability and the work of Jesus would not be necessary.

I would like to caution you that grace is not an excuse to "do whatever feels right since we can just ask for forgiveness later." The moment anyone begins to use and abuse God's grace and use it as an excuse to sin; then they are stepping into very dangerous territory. God knows the thoughts and intents of a person's heart as it relates to grace, and we cannot fool God. The writer of the Book of Hebrews strongly cautions against this going as far as saying:

"For if we go on deliberately *and* willingly sinning after once acquiring the knowledge of the Truth, there is no longer any sacrifice left to atone for [our] sins [no further offering to which to look forward]" (Hebrews 10:26 AMP).

God's ultimate purpose in the Book of Hosea is to reveal His incredible love for His people, even those who have rejected Him. Yet you also see how sternly and severely God deals with sinners when they refuse to turn from their sin.

He did not even spare His own Son and His death on the cross who had to pay the penalty of for our sins, making us righteousness so we can stand in His holy presence. Without Christ's salvation, we are separated eternally from Him.

"O Israel, return to the LORD your God, For you have stumbled because of your iniquity; ²Take words with you And return to the LORD. Say to Him, Take away all iniquity; Receive us graciously, For we will offer the sacrifices of our lips. For in You the fatherless finds mercy. ⁴"I will heal their backsliding, I will love them freely, For My anger has turned away from him. ⁹Who is wise? Let him understand these things. Who is prudent? Let him know them. For the ways of the LORD are right; The righteous walk in them, But transgressors stumble in them" (Hosea 14).

It is important to grasp the love of God. He presents Himself in the Book of Hosea as a "Husband." He wants us to realize that the ways of sin are spiritual adultery and perdition. This story reveals the rebellion of the people, who are oblivious as they strive against God's ways. It concludes by disclosing how committed our loving, and faithful God is to us, His wayward bride —

> "…Adulterers and adulteresses! Do you not know that friendship with the world is enmity with God? Whoever, therefore, wants to be a friend of the world makes himself an enemy of God. Or do you think that the Scripture says in vain, The Spirit who dwells in us yearns jealously…" (James 4:1-5)?

Below is a passage from the Book of Hosea that deeply touches my heart. The Lord opens up and exposes the vulnerability of His heart for us unfaithful ones. What an indescribable demonstration of love! My mind cannot fathom His love. We humans are too sensitive, too obstinate, and inflexible. Our love is compromised, quick and easy. I am in awe of His great love; even when we are sinners, He loves us. (Romans 5:8) I have heard that He loved us because He foresaw that we were going to love Him. No, no and no! He foresaw our decadence and loved us despite what He saw.

God's Continuing Love for Israel

"When Israel was a child, I loved him, and out of Egypt I called My son. As they called them, so they went from them; they sacrificed to the Baals (to false gods), and burned incense to carved images. I taught Ephraim (tribe) to walk, taking them by their arms; but they did not know that I healed them. I drew them with gentle cords, with bands of love, and I was to them as those who take the yoke from their neck. I stooped and fed them...My people are bent on backsliding from Me. Though they call to the Most High; none at all exalt Him (at heart). How can I give you up, Ephraim? How can I hand you over, Israel? How can I make you like Admah? How can I set you like Zeboim? My heart churns within Me; My sympathy is stirred. I will not execute the fierceness of My anger; I will not again destroy Ephraim. For I am God, and not man, The Holy One in your midst..." (Hosea 11:1-4, 7-11 AMP).

Don't think for a moment that the Lord is referring to Israel only. He opened the covenant to all who will believe. He already loved us before the "countdown" began. Consider these passages—

"Jew and Gentile are the same in this respect. They have the same Lord, who gives generously to all who call on him" (Romans 10:12 NLT).

"There is no longer Jew or Gentile, slave or free, male and female. For you are all one in Christ Jesus" (Galatians 3:28 NLT).

"In this new life, it doesn't matter if you are a Jew or a Gentile, circumcised or uncircumcised, barbaric, uncivilized, slave, or free. Christ is all that matters, and he lives in all of us" (Colossians 3:11 NLT).

I am convinced that we are to acknowledge this infinite love of our marvelous and sweet God. He is a father to the fatherless, a mother to the orphan, a husband to the widow, and for the bride. He cares immensely for us. He is interested in what interests us; concerned with what concerns us, and in what causes us sorrow. Our victories are His victories.

Many take issue with the freedom He has given each of us to choose death or life. I know that it is hard to assimilate sometimes. We need to understand the highest privilege that the Lord gives us is to be born free. Freedom is the mark of our true value to Him, a worth so profound that we couldn't be born slaves. Freedom is the highest honor the Lord has given us, but with freedom comes big responsibilities. With the same freedom we choose to live for sin, we can choose to live for Him!

My Son Killed Himself

Chapter Eight
EYES ARE OPENED

Jorge's Personal Encounters with God

I remember Jorge trying to find a way to have a relationship with the Lord at a very young age. My parents did their best to teach my brother and me the necessity of experiencing God every day. My parents also taught Jorge that there was a God to whom he should submit his life. A God with the power to righteously judge and redeem sinners by completely removing their sins forever, or casting them out of His holy presence for all eternity. We explained to Jorge that God (the Great I AM) would save those who are cleansed by the blood of Jesus Christ. We told him about the power of His resurrection and that salvation only comes for those who approach Him with sincere repentance.

Train Up a Child

My mother did a great job with Jorge from ages 5 to 8 years old. She took him to church on Sundays, made sure that he took his first communion and that he went to confession when he realized he had sinned against God, his Maker, and final Judge. I thank my parents for their effort and works of faith. They were not in vain the Word of God tells us:

My Son Killed Himself

"Train up a child in the way he should go, and when he is old will not depart from it" (Proverbs 22:6).

Salvation Every Sunday

When Jorge was eleven years old, he spent the whole year here in the United States. For the first time, he finished the school year in one single place. During that year, we also attended Second Baptist Church in Houston pastored by Dr. Ed Young. Jorge loved it and asked me to please take him to Bible Study on Wednesday nights and the main service on Sunday mornings.

He attended Vacation Bible School one summer with his friends and he loved it. Many Sundays, when we would attend the Sunday service, he would ask me to walk to the front so we could accept Jesus as our Lord and our Savior, which I did, partly for him. He even wanted to be baptized and be a member of the church.

Looking back, I realize that this is one of the areas in Jorge's life that I neglected because of my arrogance and ignorance. I have asked myself a thousand times what would have happened if I had done what he asked. What if we had become members of the church? "I am a Catholic," I would tell myself. I was certainly not going to sell out my true doctrine for a church without any "traditions" and especially a church with no Pope. How blind, I was!

Seeking a Sign from God

Years later, when Jorge was lost in sin, he always looked for a sign from God in his life. I remember one time when he went to the Mardi Gras festival in New Orleans. His intention was to party hard and wild. Instead, he wound up in a Christian booth, speaking for hours to a Spirit-filled Christian woman who was there doing an evangelistic outreach from a church in Alabama.

We have to admit, and please do not feel offended when I call it as it is but when you remove the "mask" of Mardi Gras it has become nothing more than a festival of debauchery. Drunkenness, nakedness, immorality, and wild behavior are the norm. They are not only commonplace but celebrated publicly on the street. I am far from being an antiquity, in fact, those who know me know that I believe in "having fun." However, "having fun" doesn't mean I must sin to do so. Now is not a time to shrink in cowardice. I must stand strong and speak the truth. I will do so in love, but I speak nonetheless.

For years, following his trip, Jorge would spend hours talking with her on the phone. I became a friend with her as well. When I found out about the experience he had at Mardi Gras and what had happened, I remembered a moment I had years before. I had bowed down in my bedroom and prayed to the Lord to be where I couldn't be, to reach, and to have a voice when I couldn't speak. I firmly believe she was God's answer to my prayer as I know "…the prayers of a righteous person are powerful and effective" (James 5:16).

As the years passed, Jorge's rebellious ways grew more constant, and he began to make quite a name for himself. He was "living for the moment." Darkness provided him with many followers who thought as he thought and did what he did. They too wanted to do it, and do it now; to have it, and have it now. They lived to fulfill their desires for the moment without regret. Nevertheless, this type of living is a lie. It's not a "lifestyle;" it's really a "deathstyle." Sooner or later regrets do arrive. They embraced and lived by the attitude, "Live for the moment because you only live once." That attitude led to so much destruction.

Bread of Life

My husband, Jorge's brother and I will never forget the day in 2009 when Jorge went to church with us. At this time, we were attending Bread of Life Church (now New Life Church) Pastored by Dusty Kemp in Houston, Texas. We were sitting close to the front that Sunday, and worship was phenomenal. I was overwhelmed with joy to have both of my sons with me. I got up from my chair and went to the front altar to worship near the pulpit. I remember bowing down before the Lord and crying so hard with gratitude.

Suddenly, my younger son joined me, and a few minutes later, Jorge. He cried, hugged me and whispered in my ear asking for forgiveness. He bowed and prayed. He worshiped and cried with all his heart. At the end of the service, Jorge walked to the front to accept the Lord Jesus as his Savior and waited to speak with Pastor Kemp. They spoke for well over 20 minutes and afterward Pastor Kemp approached us and told us that God was working very strong in Jorge's heart. That day Jorge was also ministered by two other men at the altar before we left.

I don't know what happened between God and Jorge. I don't know if Jorge was born again that day, but I know for a fact that he had a head-on encounter with God over his lifestyle of sin. I am also certain that Jorge recognized that a relationship with the Lord Jesus was central to salvation. He knew about Heaven and hell, right and wrong, and salvation for all who repent and turn from their sins. Of course, every demon in hell rebelled against the encounter Jorge had that day as they recognize the position and authority of the Lord. Only God knows the contents of a man's heart.

I marvel at God's grace and infinite love, which is beyond imagination. How can I expect so much goodness when I fall? How can I conceive the magnitude of His love? How could I understand His judgments? It brings to mind one of my favorite Bible passages written by the Apostle Paul that says:

"For this reason I bow my knees to the Father of our Lord Jesus Christ, from whom the whole family in Heaven and earth is named, that He would grant you, according to the riches of His glory, to be strengthened with might through His Spirit in the inner man, that Christ may dwell in your hearts through faith; that you, being rooted and grounded in love, may be able to comprehend with all the saints what is the width and length and depth and height—to know the love of Christ which passes knowledge; that you may be filled with all the fullness of God" (Ephesians 3:14-19 NKJV).

Our Father's profound love toward us is unquestionable, unchangeable, unquenchable and extravagant. How can He love us so much?

He offers us such an amazing and precious promise in the Book of Chronicles—"If My people, who are called by My Name, shall humble themselves, pray, seek, crave, and require of necessity My face and turn from their wicked ways, then will I hear from Heaven, forgive their sin, and heal their land" (2 Chronicles 7:14 AMP).

If you feel led by the Lord, pray this simple prayer with me:

"Lord Jesus, I accept you from this day forward as my Lord and only Savior. Forgive my sins; cleanse my heart, and renew my mind through the power of your Word. Give me a new life with you Lord. I crave it desperately. I do. Guide and protect me, my Shepherd, especially now that I am rejecting the work of the enemy in my life.

Today, at this moment, I renounce the work of Satan's kingdom in my life, mind, desires, will and heart. Strengthen me, Lord. May your thoughts become my thoughts, and your ways become my ways, that your heart may become my heart.

Lord, give me eyes to see as you see, and ears to hear your voice. Holy Spirit, make yourself strong inside of me, speak clearly to me so I can choose life over death. In Jesus' name I pray. Amen."

(Now read: Isaiah 55:6-12)

Never forget that the Lord God Almighty sent His only Son to save sinners, to find the lost sheep, to bring His Life to the dead and His Light to dispel the darkness. His Son came to comfort the brokenhearted and to set the captives free.

I rejoice every time I recall Mark (2:17) as Jesus explains His mission to the Pharisees. He said, "It is not the healthy who needs a doctor, but the sick. I have not come to call the righteous, but sinners." Apart from Him, no one is in good spiritual health. He penetrates the arrogant egos of those deceiving themselves thinking that they have no need of restoration.

What an amazing way that Jesus launched His ministry. He stood up in the Synagogue, He was handed the scroll of Prophet Isaiah, He unrolled the scroll and found the place where it was written (prophesied about Him)—

> "The Spirit of the Lord [is] upon Me, because He has anointed Me [the Anointed One, the Messiah] to preach the good news (the Gospel) to the poor; He has sent Me to announce release to the captives and recovery of sight to the blind, to send forth as delivered those who are oppressed [who are downtrodden, bruised, crushed, and broken down by calamity], To proclaim the accepted *and* acceptable year of the Lord [the day when salvation and the free favors of God profusely abound]. Then He rolled up the book and gave it back to the attendant and sat down; and the eyes of all in the synagogue were gazing [attentively] at Him. And He began to speak to them: Today this Scripture has been fulfilled while you are present *and* hearing" (Luke 4:18-19 AMP).

During the last year of Jorge's life, he would drive many of his "friends" insane when they would ride in his car with him. He would play the song "Jesus, Take the Wheel" by Carrie Underwood, incessantly. Throughout his final days on earth, with a pure brokenness of heart perhaps more real than ever before, Jorge came to understand and was truly convinced that he needed a Savior. He never thought, expected or understood the infinite love of God. He couldn't conceive of God's vast understanding of a person's heart and broken and delusional mind. How then could God do the unthinkable and grant Jorge eternity in Heaven?

After meditating and seeking the Lord, I have determined that above all, God loved Jorge more than I ever could. I am fully persuaded based on a covenant that God established in His infinite wisdom and love for Jorge, made provision for Jorge. I know he was given multiple occasions to recognize and accept Jesus many times prior to taking his life. Despite the fact that his mind had most likely gone into a deep delusional state and had lost touch with reality.

It is God's promise for righteous families who represent the Lord on earth that our family will be saved! "Believe in the Lord Jesus, and you will be saved—you and your household" (Acts 16:31).

We, mothers, wives, fathers, husbands, children have a lot of power given to us because of this covenant. If we are born again and believers in the Lord Jesus Christ then we have the power and authority to use the Name of Jesus. We are covered with and by His blood and invited to boldly approach His throne. We are seated with Him in the Heavenly places according to the Book of Ephesians (2:6) putting all enemies under His feet. He makes intercession for us and our love ones against principalities and dominions in the highest and darkest places.

Without a doubt, God's unquenchable and eternal love and mercy for Jorge (as a child of a righteous woman and covenant family) gave him the opportunity to recognize the sovereignty and omnipotence of God. Even as his mind was vanishing, and darkness was coming to take his life, but not his spirit. I rejoice in this fact!

Hours before Jorge's Death

On multiple occasions through the years, God has awakened me out of a sound sleep to speak to me as His daughter. I typically journal these moments of impartation spent with the Lord. On March 8th, 2011 at 10:47 p.m., I was awakened by the Lord, which at the time did not seem unusual since that is how God chooses to get my undivided attention. I was completely unaware of the significance what had taken place on that night until nearly a month after Jorge's death.

I cannot remember if I got out of bed that night or stayed in bed. But one thing is certain, as He began to speak to me, and I began to write, He led me first to the Book of Psalms where I read:

"Thus my heart was grieved, and I was vexed in my mind. I was so foolish and ignorant; I was like a beast before You.

Nevertheless, I am continually with You; You hold me by my right hand. You will guide me with Your counsel, and afterward receive me to glory. Whom have I in Heaven but You? And there is none upon earth that I desire besides You. My flesh and my heart fail; but God is the strength of my heart and my portion forever" (Psalms 73: 21-26 NKJV).

At the same time that I wrote a portion of Psalm 73, the Holy Spirit prompted me to write and proclaim the following words about my family —

"Tonight I declare my freedom and the freedom of my family from any type of bondage, chains, and oppression. I specifically declare my son's and family's independence from the shackles and persecution of darkness. I declare FREEDOM from demonic influences and in one voice with God's Spirit I say NO MORE! No more bondage for us and no more bondage for my son, Jorge. I declare our freedom and independence from this oppression today, freedom from demonic intervention in our lives... In Jesus' name, Amen."

When this time of God's impartation had ended, I went back to sleep and did not remember what I had written while under the influence of the Holy Spirit. That impartation God gave me was one day before my son would take his life. It was only one month later that I found the note and realized that it had occurred the day before my beloved Jorge died.

It was a month later that I understood meaning and depth of the passage given to me from Psalm 73:21. I suddenly knew that it wasn't given to me about myself, as I initially believed. Instead, the Lord had done the unthinkable. He had shared with me the intimate thoughts coming from deep within Jorge's heart as he started to descend to a point of no return. Do I want to believe in these connections because I am Jorge's mother, perhaps? However, I think it's much more than that. In fact, those who know me well, know that if I had to write that Jorge went to hell, I would have done so as painful as it would be. My assignment is to speak the truth about the glorious righteousness of God without offering excuses or apologies. However, through the death of my son, I have learned more about God's victories over darkness, about His love toward sinners, and about His amazing grace!

I am not the judge of my son's eternal destiny. That is all in God's hands, but I will repeat it once again that only God knows the last cry from a person's heart!

This is why it is imperative that we minister the Word of the Lord to our loved ones and never compromise with them. Not in their sin, and not in their living outside the boundaries that God has set for man. Speaking the truth of the Gospel of

Christ in an open, respectful, and honest way is our only hope for their salvation. We need to consistently pray for our family, friends and our *enemies* lifting them up to God daily, interceding for their salvation. Never forget that in the Book of Isaiah (43:16-19) God said "He would make a way in the sea, a path through the mighty waters, a road in the wilderness and rivers in the desert" and that we must trust that the He will make a way even when there doesn't seem to be any conceivable way.

My Son Killed Himself

Chapter Nine
THE VISIT

Many years prior to Jorge's death; the Lord gave me a vision of my son that I held onto so tightly. It was a vision of my son returning to me, and turning to God—a vision of restoration and renewal. A vision that was so vivid and so real that I can still close my eyes and see it to this day.

My mother and I were in the midst of a very large estate with the most beautiful castle we have ever seen. The estate was encircled by a very tall and ornately detailed stone wall, within which were three main courtyards, each on three different levels. The courtyards had meticulously sculpted beautiful gardens. Each level was separated by a 4 ½ foot stone wall and five very long and wide stone steps.

Suddenly my mother and I we were on the second level, which was also the middle of the three courtyards. To our backs was the first level, an outer courtyard, and it was also the lowest of the three levels. It had the largest garden of the three with beautiful plants and flowers throughout. We were facing the top level, the third courtyard, which was the smallest of the three. The castle also sat on this level. This third higher courtyard had the most beautiful plants with flowers in abundance.

The mid-level second courtyard, where my mother and I stood, was the most exquisite of the three. Everywhere we looked were pure white roses, as if we were surrounded. We each held a basket, in our hand and we were trimming those extraordinary white roses and placing them in our baskets. I noticed that they had no thorns.

The sun shone brightly over my mother and me. It was the most amazing feeling as if we were taking a bath in sunlight. It was a miraculously gorgeous day!

The rose bushes that we were trimming next to the 4 ½ foot stone wall that separated the first and second courtyards. This particular courtyard (middle) had a stone walkway that ran the entire length east to west. At each end of the stone, the walkway was a gated door that led to the outside if one were leaving, or the inside if one were entering the estate grounds.

Suddenly, I lifted up my head toward the gated west door and I saw my son, Jorge, entering through the gate. He was not particularly well dressed and looked unkempt, wearing only jogging pants and a T-shirt. It appeared he hadn't taken a bath in quite some time, and he looked weary. As he walked toward us, he was uncommonly quiet. I sensed that after so many years, he was coming back home to his mama (me) for good this time!

I turned to my mother, who was still trimming roses, pointed in Jorge's direction and said, "Mama, look!" We immediately dropped our baskets and ran towards him to welcome him home! When we got to him we embraced him in a hug I will never forget. Then the three of us turned around and walked together towards the steps to our left that led up to the castle itself.

As we entered the castle, we were standing is this massive room. There were entries on each side of the huge room. One to the left and one to the right. Both of them had huge, thick, red velvet curtains hanging and pulled to the side by a gold rope. On the left side of the room, I also saw a display of a suit of armor, as one might typically see in castles. It was very large, probably close to eight feet tall. When I saw it, I recalled the description of "the Armor of God" as mentioned in the sixth chapter of the Book of Ephesians. Then I realized it was more than the armor of a soldier. It was the Armor of God! I turned to Jorge and said, "George is waiting for you." Jorge quietly walked to his left and exited through the door on the left side of the room, closest to the Armor.

I turned around and said, "Mom, let's go get more roses. George is going to pray for Jorge and prepare him for his royal clothes." (Cleansed by the Word)

Suddenly, the vision shifted to another room within the castle. This room was slightly smaller than the main entry hall. In it was a long table, like an altar. There was also a chair elaborately decorated, and fit for a king. As I turned to talk to my mother, she was standing at a side table, on the right side, holding a huge sword, which she was polishing it with a cloth. I was overjoyed because I believed that Jorge was finally coming back home for good. George was speaking with him to prepare him to be cleansed from his sin and saved by the Blood of Jesus. I had such confidence that a ceremony was going to take place where Jorge would be "officially dressed" as one of God's royalty; he was to become a child of the King (born again)! Then the vision ended.

Confident Assurance

As the years passed, and I did not see any signs that any change had taken place in Jorge's life and would at times become disheartened. In my discouragement, I always recalled that vision, firmly, knowing in my heart that one day my son would return. He would be dressed in the spiritual garments of the royal priesthood (come to the saving knowledge of Jesus Christ), which we are promised as children of God. I was sure this vision was given to me as a sign to wait patiently, and not to lose hope because I knew how the story would end. I needed to continue to have faith because, "God is not a man that He can lie." (Numbers 23:19; Hosea 11:9; James 1:17) I was assured that God would never give me a vision of promise like this without a significance and purpose.

When God gives to you a vision of promise like this, it is to encourage you to keep you believing in (trusting in, adhering to and relying upon) Him. It is to encourage you to hold tightly to your faith no matter the times, persecutions or tribulations because He is in control. We are to have faith and be of good courage because He has already revealed the final outcome! When the Lord gives you a promise, it is set in stone, and it will come to pass. "For all the promises of God are Yes, and in Him Amen, to the glory of God through us" (2 Corinthians 1:20).

The Visit

God's Beautiful Mosaic

Looking back now, I can see in perfect detail how the vision I was given matched what happened during those last days of my son's life on this earth. My life was shattered in a million pieces yet God was creating His own beautiful mosaic. He was giving me pieces that one day would all fit together to represent a beautiful picture of His love, grace, mercy and redemption. Once the mosaic was completed I would see all of the pieces in place and see the perfect and finished work of Christ in my son's life.

Keep in mind that the last time I saw Jorge, he was dressed exactly the way I described in the vision; disheveled and unkempt wearing jogging pants and wearing a T-shirt. This just the first piece of the mosaic confirming that Jorge had entered Heaven.

As I mentioned at the beginning of the book, my mother, and sister-in-law, arrived in Houston within 36 hours of finding out Jorge was dead. My mother, sister-in-law and I decided to go to the house where Jorge had lived as my mother, and I felt the desperate need to see the place where the body of our beloved son had laid. We did this as my husband was preparing for an intimate funeral ceremony at our home. My husband was not even aware that we were leaving the house. On our way, we received a phone call from one of my good friends, telling me that one of Jorge's friends had called her. He told her that the previous night there had been a very large "vigil" for Jorge in the front yard of the home where he had been living. Jorge's friend also mentioned that close to 400 hundred people had attended the "vigil" with many seemingly devastated by the news of his death. His friend also told her that there were many posters made with Jorge's pictures on them, and hundreds of flowers were also left for us.

As we were driving up to Jorge's house, we saw a sight as we had never seen. As we parked the car, we just sat there and looked in awe. In front of us was a panorama of posters with my beautiful Jorge's picture, and the purest white roses I have ever seen. We could see no other color, but white roses. My mom and I got out of the car and walked toward the house to pick up as many posters and roses as we could.

There were no less than 12 very large vases with huge white roses. As we began to pick up all the roses, I suddenly remembered the vision and realized this was the second confirmation that I received that Jorge had entered Heaven. As I look back, I continue to marvel at how the vision He gave me is forming a mosaic to glorify Him.

When we arrived back at home and began to prepare for Jorge's intimate ceremony, we used the white roses we had picked up, and I remembered the vision once again. I felt like the Holy Spirit was opening my spiritual eyes to what He was doing.

It was then when George tearfully told me, my mother and sister-in-law about the day when he and Jorge met in his office. He told us that he and Jorge had spoken for nearly three hours. George sensed that Jorge was conflicted between making a decision to live for God and do what's right in His sight consistently; or to continue living according to the desires of his flesh, which would certainly end in his destruction. Jorge vacillated back and forth, one moment saying he was going to continue to fight and that he would eventually overcome his addictions to Hydrocodone. Only for the next moment admitting how defeated he felt, and how terrified he was about the outcome if he continued to live in his own ability. He was scared that he wasn't going to defeat his Hydrocodone addiction. The chains he thought he had broken were still binding him. The withdrawals and desire for more were simply too overwhelming. He recognized his end would be destruction. As I mentioned earlier, how terrible is the price of ignorance! We all were blind to the real chemical bondage Jorge was experiencing in his body, his brain, and his central nervous system.

George and Jorge talked about God, eternity, salvation and eternal life and eternal condemnation. Jorge kept telling George that he didn't want to end up in hell, incapable to enter the Kingdom of the Lord, separated from His goodness forever.

At the end of their long, emotional, and intimate conversation, my husband asked Jorge if he was planning to do something irrational. Jorge knew exactly what he was referring to. He flatly said no. He said that he had attended funerals of friends who committed suicide, and saw the pain they left behind. He said he would never put me, his brother, his grandparents or George through that pain. George said that before Jorge left, they embraced tightly for at least five minutes saying Jorge cried from the deepest part of his soul, telling him over and over again, "I love you, I love you, I love you." Each time Jorge said "I love you," my husband repeated and told Jorge "I love you." Jorge repeatedly apologized for all the times he had put us through hell. Just before Jorge let go from their embrace, he told my husband that he was going to make the right decision and that my husband was going to be proud of him. That gave my husband much solace and comfort.

One thing that was very clear to George after that meeting with Jorge. He knew that Jorge was going to make a radical and profound decision to change his life, but never did he consider that Jorge would take his life.

There is not much I can say after this, but I will leave you with a few scriptures on which to meditate:

"For the desires of the flesh are opposed to the [Holy] Spirit, and the [desires of the] Spirit are opposed to the flesh (godless human nature); for these are antagonistic to each other [continually withstanding and in conflict with each other], so that you are not free but are prevented from doing what you desire to do" (Galatians 5:17 AMP).

"For the sinful nature is always hostile to God. It never did obey God's laws, and it never will" (Romans 8:7 NLT).

"And crying out with a loud voice saying, Salvation belongs to our God who sits on the Throne and to the Lamb" (Revelation 7:10 NKJV).

"For the Lord is close to the brokenhearted and saves those who are crushed in spirit" (Psalm 34:18 NIV).

My Son Killed Himself

Chapter Ten
FORGIVE & YOU WILL BE FORGIVEN

When we were growing up, my mother and father instilled in us the principle of forgiveness. It was an aspect of their lives that I admire to this day. It is dignifying, honorable, pure, but above all, it is Godly.

Every time we encountered injustices or wrongdoing from others, my mother and father always gave us one recommendation: "Bow your knees to the Lord, lift your arms to Heaven and praise Him. He will come to your rescue. There is nothing else you need to say. He will redeem you and protect you. He will bring justice, and He will deal with your enemies." My mother says to this day, "Do not allow a seed of resentment or unforgiveness to take root in your heart. Keep yourself pure. If you allow the evil doers to change you inside, they win!"

This teaching of forgiveness was planted deep in our hearts. As Jorge grew, he also carried within him the forgiveness seed, planted deep in his heart. On many occasions, especially towards the end of Jorge's life, my mom and I continued to reinforce the importance and necessity of forgiveness every time we would speak with him.

Jorge, as I said previously was very spoiled. In fact, he would acknowledge that he was a "spoiled brat." However, he also experienced many disappointments in life, and countless people let him down. He was a giver as much as a taker. Many can testify to this. Those who loved him and those who did not care that much for him, will all say that one of the things that set Jorge apart was his big forgiving heart. During these moments of his life, even as the end approached, Jorge clearly understood more than ever that he must forgive at all costs.

I remember during the last three weeks of his life speaking with him about forgiving others. Many times he complained about the people that he cared for the most and had given of himself for many years had abandoned him. He felt they abandoned him without mercy or compassion when he needed them most. Jorge cried a lot those last days many times saying what a fool he had been. Saying he had "traded the 'gold' for the 'bronze'," likening his family to 'gold' and his friends to 'bronze'.

I remember telling him the story of the unforgiving servant in the book of Matthew. I encouraged him to hold strong to that teaching. If someone needs forgiveness, we are required to forgive. Let's review this valuable and profound parable taught by our Lord —

"Therefore the kingdom of Heaven is like a human king who wished to settle accounts with his attendants. When he began the accounting, one was brought to him who owed him 10,000 talents (probably about $10,000,000), And because he could not pay, his master ordered him to be sold, with his wife and his children and everything that he possessed, and payment to be made. So the attendant fell on his knees, begging him, Have patience with me and I will pay you everything. And his master's heart was moved with compassion, and he released him and forgave him (canceling) the debt. But that same attendant, as he went out, found one of his fellow attendants who owed him a hundred denarii (about twenty dollars); and he caught him by the throat and said, Pay what you owe! So his fellow attendant fell down and begged him earnestly, give me time, and I will pay you all! But he was unwilling, and he went out and had him put in prison till he should pay the debt. When his fellow attendants saw what had happened, they were greatly distressed, and they went and told everything that had taken place to their master. Then his master called him and said to him, you contemptible and wicked attendant! I forgave and canceled all that (great) debt of yours because you begged me to. And should you not have had pity and mercy on your fellow attendant, as I had pity and mercy on you? And in wrath his master turned him over to the torturers (the jailers), till he should pay all that he owed. So also My Heavenly Father will deal with every one of you if you do

not freely forgive your brother from your heart
his offenses" (Matthew 18:23-35 AMP).

As we live our lives, we offend people as often as we are
offended. We can even hurt people unintentionally, the same
way, others can unintentionally hurt us. We are born into a
nature of sin and in a sin nature, we develop our lives. The
law of sin dwells in us and is at work in us—

"But I see another law at work in me, waging
war against the law of my mind and making me
a prisoner of the law of sin at work within me"
(Romans 7:23 NIV).

Nevertheless, we are to forgive. It is imperative that we do
so, or as the story explains, God will be forced to turn us over
to our "jailers and torturers," or as the King James Version
says, our "tormentors." Unforgiveness keeps us chained to
the person we do not forgive. As long as we choose to hold
unforgiveness we cannot be freed from jail, and we will
remain chained in bondage. Satan delights in unforgiveness,
because when we choose to not forgive then he has access to
torture the mind, will, and emotions. If we don't forgive, then
God will not forgive us.

Bondage Rooted in Unforgiveness

During one of my many conversations with Pastor Pablo Bottari, recognized as one of the worldwide deliverance ministry experts, he has shared with me some of his vast wisdom as it relates to the deliverance. He told me that the vast majority of the deliverances he has encountered with extensive bondage and oppression were rooted in either unforgiveness or witchcraft. Don't be too quick to exempt yourself from this sin of witchcraft either. According to the Scriptures, the spirit of witchcraft involves manipulation, rebellion, an unteachable spirit, stubbornness, and idolatry (including self-idolatry or the idolatry of another human being whom we elevate above God). I strongly recommend Pablo Bottari's book, *Free in Christ*.

Our Lord exhorts us to have a forgiving spirit—

"And forgive our debts, as we forgive our debtors..." (Matthew 6:9-13).

"For if you forgive men their trespasses, your Heavenly Father will also forgive you. But if you do not forgive men their trespasses, neither will your Father forgive your trespasses" (Matthew 6:14-15 NKJV).

"Then Peter came to Him and said, 'Lord, how often shall my brother sin against me, and I forgive him? Up to seven times?' Jesus said, 'I do not say to you, up to seven times, but up to seventy times seven" (Matthew 18:21-22 NKJV).

My parents wanted us to know and understand the importance of forgiveness. We cannot claim mercy, when we offer none, as happened to the servant of the King. The King was furious to learn that after he bestowed compassion to his servant and canceled his debt, the servant wouldn't practice the same principle the King showed.

Let me clarify forgiveness for you. To forgive somebody who has hurt you or sinned against you does not mean to diminish or minimize the sins that were committed against you. Nor does it mean that you deserved such treatment. Furthermore, it doesn't mean that you are to abandon your common sense or wisdom, and will simply trust the person who injured you as though nothing has happened. Nor does it mean you are to put yourself in a defenseless position to once again be hurt or injured.

Each case is different, so you must judge the person and the wrong accordingly. Trust is something that is earned by a person's conduct. It is important that you wisely determine if the one who harmed you has repented and understands the wrong they have done; or if they have not repented and had no clue of the extent of their actions. Repentance is more than just saying "I'm sorry."

True repentance is an acknowledgment that what you have done is a sin, the humility to ask God to forgive you, do an 180-degree turn and run the other direction from that sin to never commit again. That is the mindset of repentance. Just because somebody has repented and just because you have forgiven doesn't require you to reestablish a relationship with them, God still wants us to exercise wisdom.

We are commanded to forgive, and to pray for our enemies. If we find ourselves in the position to exercise compassion and kindness toward an enemy in a time of need, we must not hesitate to provide the assistance if we are able. These are attributes of the children of God. As we perform virtuous and respectable deeds toward our enemies, we bring honor and good reputation to us, and to our Father in Heaven.

We are also taught that the lack of forgiveness will become a barrier that blocks our prayers, even regarding our finances. Take a look at these Scriptures found in the Book of Matthew and Book of Psalms:

"Therefore if you bring your gift to the altar, and there remember that your brother has something against you, leave your gift there before the altar, and go your way. First be reconciled to your brother, and then come and offer your gift" (Matthew 5:23-24 NKJV).

"If I had not confessed the sin in my heart, the Lord would not have listened" (Psalm 66:18 NLT).

It is not enough that you reconcile with God. You must also make peace in your heart with the one against whom you feel animosity, resentment, or hostility. Simply put, "Let it go!" Then, you can offer your gifts, your prayers, and your service to the Lord, and He will bless them and make them prosper.

Be assured that these feelings will not come naturally or freely to you. Your flesh will oppose, reject, and fight against reconciliation and forgiveness. But this isn't about how "you feel." It's not a matter of emotion at all. It's a matter of obedience to God. Forgiveness is not an emotional experience. It's a conscious choice.

Many years ago, I was raped. I remember the traumatic effect it had on me. I hid in my parents' house for weeks. I felt dirty, lost and abused. One day someone who loved me dearly came by our house and asked if I would allow him to go and "teach a lesson" to the person who raped me. A lesson that he would never forget. The incident happened long ago, but it is still fresh in my mind. We were living in Latin America where many unlawful things are possible, if you know what I mean. For those who can afford it, the law can be "purchased."

My parents never knew about this. My answer was an absolute, "No!" Under no circumstance did I want this person harmed. Sadly, due to corruption in the legal system, the law was not going to make him pay for assaulting me. God was going to be the One, who exacted justice, not me.

A few weeks later, the priest from our neighborhood came and visited me. As I confessed any unconfessed sin, I asked him, "Father (Priest), how do I know if I hate this man or not? How do I know if I have forgiven him?"

He answered me with another question. "Jessica, if you were to find that man lying on the street bleeding, would you help him if he asked for help?"

I said tearfully, "Yes, I would."

Then he asked me, "Do you wish him harm or destruction, apart from legal justice?

I said, "No, I don't."

Then he asked, "Would you like to say along with me, 'Lord, I forgive this man?'"

I said, "Yes, I would." We prayed together.

The priest explained to me that forgiveness wasn't an emotion or something that you naturally feel. Instead, forgiveness is a decision we make unto the Lord. Sometimes we have to repeat it multiple times until we grab hold of it. The priest also clarified my feelings with these words. "What happened to you is undeniable. Your heart and your mind are tender right now. The hurt, the damage is fresh; but, little by little it will become easier for you to say, "I forgive."

Consequences of Refusing to Forgive

When we withhold forgiveness from someone, we set ourselves up to reap the same from God. How can we expect Him to forgive us if we do not forgive others? In the Lord's model prayer, He teaches us to pray, "Forgive me my sins, as I forgive those who sin against me." Most of us judge ourselves less severely than we judge others. Scripture teaches:

> "The heart is deceitful above all things and beyond cure. Who can understand it? I the LORD search the heart and examine the mind, to reward each person according to their conduct, according to what their deeds deserve" (Jeremiah 17:9-10 NIV).

Not only are we unqualified to judge the hearts of others; but we are also unaware of the condition of our hearts. One of the hardest things for us to do is to look inside ourselves objectively. We are biased when it involves our loved ones or us. We may act as innocent doves, but may harbor resentment in our hearts. God alone is the true judge of the heart. Perhaps this is why the Psalmist David, rather than search his own heart, invited the Judge of Heaven to do so when he prayed:

"Search me, God, and know my heart; test me and know my anxious thoughts. See if there is any offensive way in me, and lead me in the way everlasting" (Psalm 139:23-24 NIV).

For us to misjudge ourselves, or worse, to lie to ourselves, only delays the healing process. Unforgiveness blocks our ability to be forgiven by God so we must walk in an attitude of forgiveness and make the decision to forgive others, as difficult as it may be at times. If not then we are opening doors of unintended destruction in our lives.

Unforgiveness can lead to resentment and if not dealt with, a root of bitterness in our soul. And when bitterness takes root, the Bible says we will be defiled (Hebrews 12:15). This root of bitterness which defiles will create a stronghold and fortification of bondage in our soul (will, mind and emotions). If you have struggled to forgive others the following is a partial list of some things you may experience:

— Self-pity
— Anger/Rage
— Self-justification
— Revenge
— Resentment/Hatred
— Depression
— Discouragement/Despair
— Strife

— Insecurity
— Despondency (hopeless/sadness)
— Envy/Jealousy
— Rebellion
— Rejection of God's Spirit
— Hindered Prayers/Relationship with God Dis=
  rupted
— Difficulty Establishing/Maintaining Relation-
  ships
— Feelings of Condemnation
— Prolonged Physical Illness (not always the case)

Let's consider the words of Jesus—

"You have heard that it was said, 'You shall
love your neighbor and hate your enemy.' But I
say to you, love your enemies, bless those who
curse you, do good to those who hate you, and
pray for those who spitefully use you and
persecute you, that you may be sons of your
Father in Heaven; for He makes His sun rise on
the evil and on the good, and sends rain on the
just and on the unjust. For if you love those who
love you, what rewards have you? Do not even
the tax-collectors do the same? And if you greet
your brethren only, what do you do more than
others? Do not even the tax collectors do so?
Therefore, you shall be perfect, just as your

Father in Heaven is perfect" (Matthew 5:43-48 NKJV).

Jesus asks why we should expect to be rewarded for loving those who love us. That is not worthy of a prize, award, a trophy, or honor. To love those who love us is a reward in itself. It certainly demands no sacrifice on our part.

John, the Beloved Disciple of Jesus, put it this way—

> "And this is how we may discern [daily, by experience] that we are coming to know Him [to perceive, recognize, understand, and become better acquainted with Him]: if we keep (bear in mind, observe, practice) His teachings (precepts, commandments)...But he who hates (detests, despises) his brother [in Christ] is in darkness and walking (living) in the dark; he is straying *and* does not perceive *or* know where he is going, because the darkness has blinded his eyes" (1 John 2:3,11 AMP).

John is calling us out by saying, if you think you know the Lord, and you call yourselves His followers, yet do not submit to His teachings, you are a liar. You do not know Him because if you truly knew Him, you would do what He said to do. We were unlovable, ungrateful, lost, acting with wrong intentions at heart and always going straight toward evil doings. The Lord saw us and estimated that we were worth His paying the highest price humanity had ever known. He loved us without conditions, and this is the love we must exercise toward others.

I encourage you to take some time in private and find a Bible and open your hearts to the advice the Apostle Paul gives us in the Book of Romans (12:1-21). He deals specifically with forgiveness and our behavior toward our enemies. He ends that passage by saying, "Do not be overcome by evil, but overcome evil with good."

We must carefully evaluate every occasion when we feel mistreated or hurt by others. Never jeopardize your spiritual life by holding onto past hurts, betrayals, or grudges. I submit to you, it is not worthwhile! The only person who will pay is you. Quite frankly, our offenders and those who harm us don't put much thought into what we think. As someone rightly said, "We wouldn't be concerned about what people think of us if we realized how seldom they did."

The Lord tells us in the Book of Matthew that He will be sending us out like sheep into the world that is full of wolves. So He instructs us to be as wise as serpents but as gentle as doves (Matthew 10:16). We must let go of offenses quickly and be prepared to forgive because I can assure you we will be given every opportunity to do so. Life is an opportunity to forgive which sets us apart from the world system. It will position us exactly where we need to be with our Father in

Heaven and in a place where God will forgive us. When we behave as men and women of good will, we will have good reputations with others, and we'll bring God glory. We must be wise, trust the Lord to exercise justice on our behalf. God commands us to forgive yet we still have the choice to forgive. We must choose to forgive.

Here are some of the results we may see in our personal lives when we choose to forgive:

— God's Forgiveness
— Hope
— Joy
— Compassion
— Concern for Others
— Restoration
— Zeal for Life
— Love
— Emotional Freedom
— Temperance
— Kindness
— Peace
— Gentleness
— Patience
— Repentance
— Mercy/Grace
— Healing (physical/emotional)
— Increased Maturity and Personal Growth
— Decreased Anger/Anxiety

There are several excellent resources for those wrestling with unforgiveness. I recommend three excellent books—*Free in Christ* by Pablo Bottari, *Total Forgiveness* by R.T. Kendall, and *Bait of Satan* by John Bevere. I also urge you to find a good church where the ministry of deliverance and inner healing is available. Sadly, over the years, these powerful ministry areas have been largely neglected by the church.

Some adults suffer as a result of early childhood experiences of abandonment, neglect, and abuse. Others suffer from experiences later in life, like sexual immorality, addictions, witchcraft and many other sinful activities. No matter the experiences we must come to the place of recognition that we must forgive those who have hurt us, we must forgive ourselves and we also must realize that God will forgive us.

Walk in the Spirit

The Lord commands us to walk and live in the Spirit and not in the lusts of the flesh. To walk and live according to the Spirit means to allow the Holy Spirit, who is abiding within us to produce actively the fruits. The Holy Spirit is working within us to change us from the inside out, and as He does this work, we will see the fruits as a by-product of the work. He is doing the work within us, not us. Galatians 5:22-23 lists the fruits of the Spirit which are produced because of His active working within us. They are "love, joy, peace, long-suffering, gentleness, goodness, kindness, self-control, and faith." This series of verses also tells us that, "those who are

Christ's have crucified the flesh with its passions and desires. If we live in the Spirit, let us also walk in the Spirit. Let us not become conceited, provoking one another, envying one another." It is very evident that for those "who are Christ's" have crucified the flesh, so we need to walk according to the Spirit.

The "fruits of the flesh" are contrary to the fruit of the Spirit. When somebody walks according to their cravings and desires based on how they feel, they are only living for the moment. These fruits are the fruits that our society demands and craves and if we say anything contrary we are considered abnormal. The works of the flesh in Galatians 5:19-21 are, "adultery, fornication, uncleanness, lewdness, idolatry, sorcery, hatred, contentions, jealousies, outbursts of wrath, selfish ambitions, dissensions, heresies, envy, murders, drunkenness, revelries, and the like."

If we are Christians (those who are of Christ), then we must forgive. Let me reiterate that just as I have already established that grace is not a license to sin; forgiveness does not mean passivity to allow sin to occur in our midst. God loved (loves) all mankind enough to send Jesus to die on the cross for the purpose of saving all mankind however that does not mean that all mankind will be saved. God loves us enough to tell us the truth. I loved my son with all of my heart yet I told him the truth. If I told my son the truth, there is certainly no way I can compromise the truth of the Gospel of Jesus in this book. I encourage you, as we end this chapter, to kneel down before the Lord. Ask Him to empower you to extend forgiveness with a sincere heart.

Chapter Eleven
MY PERSONAL REVELATION

My Struggle

Around a month after Jorge passed away, I was walking around the house in prayer, worshipping God. After a few moments, I knelt down weeping with my hands uplifted. Suddenly and unexpectedly, I saw a vision (revelation) of my son, alive, minutes before he committed suicide. The Lord began to give me a detailed account of what happened to my son after his death.

My closest friends, an editor, a publisher, my husband and I have carefully, thoughtfully, prayerfully and even debated whether or not to include this chapter in the book. We have considered many factors. I have been hesitant and have carefully weighed the pros and cons of adding this personal vision.

We have struggled trying to determine what value my personal experience and vision would bring to the reader, especially those whose loved ones have also committed suicide. We can't possibly know others details, have any insight nor can we provide any truth concerning the eternal destination of their loved ones.

The considerations for not including this vision was the perspective that my personal vision is not integral to the story. It does not bring significant value to those who have already suffered the loss of a loved one to suicide. Also, this vision is private and should be interpreted (and potentially applied) only by and for the person who received it.

After all the deliberations, conversations, debating, waiting, thinking, and praying I have made the decision to include my personal vision and visitation from the Lord. One might ask, why was it so important to me to do so?

The primary reason for adding my personal vision to this book is I am convinced that God has told me to. I have a compelling conviction that I believe will help readers understand the magnitude of God's love, mercy, faithfulness and justice that passes all understanding and comprehension.

Through the vision I received, I rediscovered, reevaluated and had a deeper revelation of God's love, mercy, faithfulness and justice. Each of these crucial factors, were focal points in my healing process, and solidified my faith and hope in God.

Even though my vision applies directly to me, it has provided hope to my entire family. I am convinced that it will also bring hope to others that read and hear it, even if they may not receive the same vision. One of the profound aspects of the vision disclosed to me was God's covenant. The word covenant is a word that we are largely unfamiliar with in our culture. I have learned through this process that all of the preconceived ideas I had about the character of God the Father were quite shallow compared to the reality of who He is. His insight, knowledge, wisdom, and love are far greater than ours, and it's in the genuineness of God's character and glory in which we find our hope.

Before deciding to put the vision in the book I needed to answer - Can the vision that God gave me be applicable and relevant for someone else and bring them comfort and hope?

Many of us no doubt wonder if it's even possible that they went to Heaven, rather than to hell. I am convinced that it can apply to any of us who has a loved one who has taken their life.

Love and Mercy of God

"For God so loved the world that He gave His only begotten Son, that whoever believes in Him should not perish but have everlasting life" (John 3:16 NKJV).

"Much more then, having now been justified by His blood, we shall be saved from wrath through Him" (Romans 5:9 NKJV).

His Faithfulness

"But you, O Lord, are a compassionate and gracious God, slow to anger, abounding in love and faithfulness" (Psalms 86:15 NIV).

"Let us hold unswervingly to the hope we profess, for He who promised is faithful" (Hebrews 10:23 NIV).

The Justice of God

"Nothing in all creation is hidden from God's sight. Everything is uncovered and laid bare before the eyes of him to whom we must give account" (Hebrews 4:13 NIV).

After summing up these Scriptures, I will answer you who desperately ask the questions above. Is it possible for your loved one who took their life to make it to Heaven?

Yes! It is possible for our loved ones to enter Heaven. It is possible that right now they are with the Lord as their Savior. Using our finite minds, our understanding of God's covenant is very limited. But His Word is not limited. His ways are infinitely beyond our human understanding. Our limited understanding of God and His covenant is the exact reason I have chosen to add the vision God gave me to this book. I pray it will give you comfort, hope, and fuel your faith in God who is compassionate toward our sorrows, our chaotic minds, and who judges righteously.

The Word of God tells us—

"As the east is from the west, so far has He removed our transgressions from us. As a Father pities His children, so the Lord pities those who fear Him. For He knows our frame; He remembers that we are dust" (Psalm 103:12-14 NKJV).

"Because of the LORD's great love we are not consumed, for his compassions never fail" (Lamentations 3:22 NIV).

"For the word of God is alive and active. Sharper than any double-edged sword, it penetrates even to dividing soul and spirit, joints and marrow; it judges the thoughts and attitudes of the heart" (Hebrews 4:12 NIV).

God's ways are far above our ways, and His thoughts are far above our thoughts. He sees beyond the current state of our loved ones' mind. He sees beyond their hopelessness, pain, sorrow and anguish of their soul as darkness approached and snatched their lives. God has the wisdom, knowledge, understanding and discernment to see the things that we cannot see. He sees a person's heart and can easily separate their suffering and torment of their soul (will, mind and emotions) from their spirit (inner man). At the instant, they cry out to Him. No matter the moment they cry out to Him, even an instant before their death; as long as they receive the salvation of Jesus Christ.

In our limited human wisdom, we can neither understand nor discern a person's true heart and mind to judge what happened in the last moments of their life. If they called, cried out, repented, claimed, accepted the Lord Jesus Christ with a pure and contrite heart then we can have the hope that they received their salvation.

For a detailed biblical study on suicide I recommend one by Pastor Jack Hayford titled, *The Sin of Suicide*. You can find it on his website: www.jackhayford.com.

Final Answers

The questions are:

Is suicide the unpardonable sin?

No, it is not. The only unpardonable sin is to blaspheme the Holy Spirit. "Whoever speaks against (blaspheme) the Holy Spirit will not be forgiven in this life or in the eternal life to come" (Matthew 12:31-32).

Can a person who has committed suicide be in hell?

Absolutely Yes! Each of us has a limited number of tomorrows and in fact we are only certain of the breath we just took. Tomorrow is never guaranteed so to spend eternity with God in Heaven and escape eternity in hell, God does require certain things of us. We must confess with our mouth the Lord Jesus Christ and believe (trust in, adhere to, rely upon) in our hearts that He rose from the dead. We must repent of our sin, and accept Jesus Christ, the King of Kings and Lord of Lords as our Lord. (Romans 10:9, 10-13) That can, and often does, happen in an instant. But let me assure you, it is not worth taking the chance.

The Vision

God's Mercy: Vision Following Jorge's Death

The days following Jorge's death were foggy to say the least. I was devastated and barely able to function. The only thing I had to stand on was the unwavering trust I had in God's righteous judgments, which are according to His character. My confidence was in Him. I knew in my heart that the Lord is a good Judge, He is trustworthy and omniscient. He who has complete knowledge, awareness, and understanding. He is the One, who perceives all things. I trusted Him and I became willing to accept His righteous judgment in the matter.

After Jorge had died, we immediately began to receive several confirmations about his eternal destiny. My husband George perceived one in his spirit. A trusted friend, who is a mighty person of prayer, called us the day after we discovered Jorge had died. She spoke with George first, because I was in my bedroom with people ministering to me non-stop. George entered the bedroom and said, "Baby, you need to take this call."

He handed me the phone, and she began to tell me what she had already told my husband. She was in prayer when she saw Jorge enter Heaven. Jorge's younger brother, received a vision at church, the first Sunday after Jorge died. For a second, he caught a glimpse of his brother standing behind the pulpit, during worship. Jorge was smiling, clapping, and singing to the Lord. I also received several Scriptures by the Holy Spirit to Biblically clarify how Jorge entered the Kingdom.

There were a few other distinct events that transpired, which I will treasure in my heart. Through all these visions, I knew in my heart that God my Father and holder of my covenant of salvation had not forsaken or abandoned me, or Jorge.

The Lord has been kind and merciful toward me communicating some of the details of my son's departure. It is with this expectant hope that I open my heart to you to reveal the events that transpired when my son took his life. I pray that through what I am about to share you can grasp the marvelous greatness of the Lord's mercy toward us. If you are going through similar anguish and pain, my deep desire is that the Lord will comfort you as he has comforted me.

My Vision, My Hope

One day after Jorge's death, I was worshiping the Lord, and thanking Him for His kindness. I wept and thanked Him over and over for being by my side through the worst experience of my life; at the moment when I needed His presence and companionship the most, He was there. I could feel Him around me, carrying me through this tragedy. When I was almost dead in His arms, He held me tightly, close to His heart. I felt that the only way I could live with the pain was in His arms. I was thanking Him for His goodness and mercy. He had appeared to my son at the end of his life. I couldn't believe how He was able to save my son from eternal damnation, given his life was so errant and chaotic. He was a true Father to the fatherless!

Suddenly and unexpectedly, I saw a vision of Jorge in his bedroom, crying and walking around his credenza with a gun in his hand. I sensed so much confusion and darkness in that room; yet at the same time, I sensed the overwhelming presence of the Lord there. It astounded me. It was as if God's angels were waiting there, but at a distance, queued up, waiting to act. It was a bizarre picture, difficult for me to understand.

Soon I saw him walking toward his walk-in closet, and suddenly I heard a gunshot. I wasn't allowed to see the event itself. The next thing I saw was Jorge's body hit the floor; while simultaneously his spirit exited his body. Mirroring the position of his body on the floor, yet in a vertical position, literally hovering above his dead body. His "spirit body" stood mid-center of his dead body, looking toward his feet. He seemed completely confused, realizing that though he should be dead, he was somehow awake and conscious. He was aware he had killed himself but was confused because he was still there, alive! These events happened rapidly.

Seconds later, I saw two demons appear near the physical feet of his dead body. Gnarled and ashy black, standing next to one another they stretched out their arms to take possession of my son's spirit. Merely three feet away from him, looking straight at him, they were obviously confident of their catch.

Immediately, Jorge's face was filled with fear at the sight of them, but as quickly as his face turned to fear, an angel of the Lord appeared at Jorge's right side, and said, "Do not be afraid." Then the angel turned to the demons and said, "Whosoever calls on the name of the Lord will not be put to shame." (Romans 10:11) The angel said it simply, and calmly; but yet with authority and dominion in his voice.

There was no battle for the angel to fight. He turned halfway around, and Jorge moved with him at the same time, now facing the head of his dead body on the floor. Suddenly, there was another angel on his left, and a third angel to his back. Jorge looked quite confused as he watched what was happening. Then a very soft, small golden light appeared in front of the three of them, which I knew in my heart was the Spirit of the Lord.

Immediately, they launched into the air, flying away from earth. The speed at which they traveled is impossible to explain. I could neither see nor feel the speed, but knew they were traveling much faster than I could comprehend. They were following the golden light as a guide, which became brighter as they moved. The angels were protecting Jorge while traveling from earth to eternity, one angel on his right, one on his left, and one at his back. They were in the same formation they had assumed as they were above his dead body in the closet.

Suddenly, they were in front Heaven's massive gate. I couldn't see the gate clearly, but I could tell it was very large. I only saw a small section of it. Then I saw two angels at the gate, holding a book. They looked at him as he approached. The angel on Jorge's left, who had previously told him "Do not be afraid" took two steps forward and said in a soft voice, "Whoever calls on the name of the Lord will be saved." (Romans 10:11) The angels at the gates nodded their heads in agreement.

The three angels accompanied Jorge through the gate. The moment Jorge passed the gate, he finally understood that he had somehow been accepted into the Kingdom of God. He was now on Holy ground, and I could see an immediate release of his effervescent, excitable personality. He turned and spoke to the angel on the left, "My mom, my mom, she has to know!" The angel turned to Jorge, smiled and calmly said, "She will know."

I then saw a large group of people approaching in the distance. I could not see their faces, or make out who they were, but I knew they were coming to welcome Jorge, and to celebrate his arrival. The angels stood still beside Jorge as the people moved closer to greet him.

After this, the same angel turned around towards me, his face right in front of mine, I was in shock. He told me that Jorge was now going to a place where he was to be cleansed and dressed with priestly garments; and that the Lord Jesus was waiting for him once he was properly attired for eternity. He also told me that there would be tears shed; but that these would be the last tears Jorge would ever cry.

They would be no tears of pain or torment, but tears of joy, happiness, and comfort mingled with tears of regret. Tears for not having served the King of Kings on earth and fulfilling his mission as a child of God. Due to this, Jorge would cry tears of repentance in front of Jesus Christ. But at the same time I was told in my spirit that Jesus himself was going to remove the tears from his face forever! God so lovingly reminded me of one of His incredible promises in the Book of Revelation—

"And God will wipe away every tear from their eyes; there shall be no more death, nor sorrow nor crying. There shall be no more pain, for the former things have passed away. Then

He who sat on the throne said, Behold, I make
all things new" (Revelation 21:4 NKJV).

The death of my precious son shattered everything I knew
into a million pieces. When God gave me this vision, it was as
if I could suddenly see the mosaic as one beautiful
masterpiece. Suddenly all of the pieces had now come
together. All of the things God had been revealing to me,
piece by piece, forming a beautiful picture of hope
consummated through this personal vision. I can now see the
perfect work of Christ completed within my son in the
mosaic. God is so faithful and just.

I would like to leave, quoting the Apostle Paul, from the
Book of Romans:

> "...The message is near you, in your mouth
> and in your heart. This is the message of faith
> that we proclaim: if you confess with your
> mouth, "Jesus is Lord," and believe in your
> heart that God raised Him from the dead, you
> will be saved. With the heart one believes,
> resulting in righteousness, and with the mouth
> one confesses, resulting in salvation...no one
> who believes on Him will be put to shame...For
> everyone who calls on the name of the Lord will
> be saved" (Romans 10:9-13 NIV).

My Son Killed Himself

Chapter Twelve

REALITY OF SUICIDE

Disclaimer: I am not a medical professional. The following is not to provide medical advice, professional diagnosis, opinion, treatment or services to you or to any other individual. The information provided in this book is not a substitute for medical or professional care, and you should not use the information in place of a visit, call, consultation, or the advice of your physician or other healthcare provider.

If you believe you have a medical emergency, you should immediately call 911 or your physician.

People who contemplate suicide, according to clinical psychologists, are desperately crying out for attention and help. These attempts, or threats of making an attempt, should not be overlooked. These individuals should be watched and analyzed by the experts on this matter. Experts usually have the training and experience to determine if the threat is for emotional manipulation or to provoke fear to exert control over others. Other times the person might be dealing with depression, an extreme sense of dread, fear, hopelessness, or worthlessness.

These factors can only be analyzed by a professional. It is imperative that parents, family, and friends find help and intervene as quickly as possible. There are times that the person who is threatening to take their life will reject the help, and resist professional intervention.

There are other individuals, who are on the verge of suicidal thoughts; who out of pure negligence for their emotional status, assume they can manage their depression, hopelessness, and sadness.

If you are in this place, I beg you to reconsider and to seek professional assistance, including spiritual and psychological counseling, as soon as possible.

Tragically, many in this condition are overconfident. You never know when your suppressed pain, or your sense of hopelessness can kill you. A large number of people who commit suicide do so because they have reached a point where they have lost all hope. There is nothing worse hopelessness!

Reportedly, the clinical factors for those who have committed suicide include:

— Profound depression

— Sense of loss (could be a relationship, a lifestyle, health, or a job)

— Anxiety

— Hopelessness or clinical factors (Central Nervous System damage)

— Severe mental illness

— Substance abuse

In recent years, we have seen a dramatic increase in abuse of prescription drugs including pain killers (opiates and other narcotics), anti-depressants, sleeping pills, anti-anxiety, etc. An increase in suicide rates and deaths from these types of medications due to overuse and addiction has occurred, raising questions. Whether due to abuse, medical errors or unethical practices, this has become an epidemic that must be addressed.

Non-prescription drugs and might I add, illegal drugs such as cocaine, crack, ecstasy, LSD, opium, bath salts and heroin are now being rebranded by the liberal media as "recreational drugs." These drugs have a direct link to the commission of crimes, countless suicides and other deaths including murder.

In my son's case, physical and psychological issues of addiction, depression, hopelessness and deep sorrow were all present when he died, and there is no doubt these were some of the main contributors to it.

Others who have, like my son, committed suicide, were under the emotional pressure of a huge sense of loss, and the inability to think straight or to use common sense. For the most part, they lost touch with reality and were overcome with fear, sorrow, regret, grief, despair, helplessness, worthlessness, and a host of other issues. One can get to a point when their pain reaches such a magnitude that the fear of dying is mitigated because it is seen as freedom from the pain.

Most people who commit suicide don't want to die. They simply don't want to live as they are. They are looking for relief from their devastating and overwhelming pain, and in their delusion most of them conclude that no one can help them. Suicide is a permanent solution to a temporary problem.

A major contributing factor to suicide is PTSD (Post-Traumatic Stress Disorder), a fracture of the mind, where the stress that an average person would ordinarily be able to handle becomes impossible to manage. PTSD affected individuals experience intense nightmares, severe anxiety, sense of loss of life as it once was. It may include flashbacks from past events that disarmed you, with many other symptoms.

For more information goto:

www.medicinenet.com
www.knowyourdose.org
www.dbsalliance.org
www.samhsa.gov

Wrong Turn, Stop!

I dedicate this portion of the book to those who are contemplating suicide in an attempt to escape your present problems. I wish to warn you that no matter how hopeless you may feel, suicide is still not the answer. It is a radical and irreversible choice. Your life will be settled, completed, and definite. It will have devastating and eternal consequences with no more chances for you. Please understand, those consequences are much worse than your current situation.

Consider the following:

— First, you have no certainty of where you will be for all eternity. You stand a great chance to spend perpetuity separated from God's goodness and benefits, in an eternal place of torment, later to wind up in the lake of fire. (Revelation 20:14) That sounds very harsh, but that is a reality. I am trying to prevent you from making the worst decision you will ever make.

— Second, the horrendous and tormenting pain that you will engrave in your loved ones is beyond your imagination. Their lives will be shattered, and they will deal with lifelong grief, on top of the perpetual regrets they will have to endure for not having had an opportunity to help you. You would not want to inflict this type of pain, even on your worst enemy. I assure you that they would never wish to inflict this type of pain on you.

You need to realize that the greatest pain your loved one will experience will not be by the hand of a stranger, but by the hand of one they love. Consider your best friends, your parents, your grandparents, your siblings and others who deeply love and care for you. They will be severely devastated by your suicide. If you are angry with your loved one and your intention is to "inflict pain on them" let me assure that this is not the answer. That emotion will pass.

When you are in pain, as you may be now, you can feel overwhelmed and hopeless. There are those that you love and care for; those who are close to your heart. Consider them first, instead of yourself and make the right choice for them. Because of your love for them, make the powerful and strong decision to overcome whatever it is you are going through. Seek assistance and tell as many people as possible who you know and trust what you are feeling and that you are considering suicide. You will discover that people care for you, and you are loved. Your mind will lie to you, do not trust it.

— Third, I know hopelessness tells you that you cannot overcome your pain, telling you there is no possibility in your tomorrow. This is a lie that your mind tells you and a trick your emotions are playing on you. It feels all too real at the moment, but I promise you this, there is hope in your tomorrow. Do not listen to the lies your mind are telling you and don't fall for the tricks your emotions are playing on you.

Please allow me to review with you two of the many great examples you will find in the Bible of people who suffered unimaginable pain. Job and King David (the Psalmist) were persecuted for years. Job by Satan himself and David by Saul and his armies. Both of them were betrayed by their friends and their loved ones.

Job had lost everything. He was finished, according to his wife. She even encouraged him encouraged him to "curse God and die." His body was covered with painful boils; his heart was devastated by the consuming pain of having lost his children, his reputation, and his finances all in the same day. His life was reduced to little more than shame, disgrace, and sorrow. Yet Job knew the character of the God that he served and in the face of all hopelessness he proclaimed:

"Though he slay me, yet will I hope in Him,
I will surely defend my ways to His face" (Job 13:15 NIV).

In the case of David, he was hiding in caves, wandering in enemy territory, unable to sleep at night for the uncertainty of his life. For years, he was brutally and unjustly persecuted. Many of the Psalms that we cherish today were written by David during these years of uncertainty. David confessed and professed that his hope was in the Lord. A faithful God, who doesn't abandon those who cry out to Him and take refuge in Him. He knew God would deliver him and give him new life.

Both of these men trusted the Lord and knew that God was just and merciful. Neither of them focused on their present painful circumstances, but instead, they kept their eyes on the Lord of their salvation. I highly recommend reading from the book of Psalms when you feel down and in despair.

I also urge you to read Mary Baxter's book, *Divine Revelation of Hell*, and Bill Wiese's book, *23 Minutes in Hell*. Hell is real, do not be deceived! There are countless Scriptures describing this horrendous place.

If you believe that a loving God is incapable of sending you to this place called hell; you are right! God is not willing that any should perish (spend eternity in hell). However, He provides you with the opportunity to choose where you will spend eternity. God is Holy. Because of this, the burning fire of His holiness protects the holy ground of His kingdom. Holiness emanates from Him. His essence is holiness as a consuming fire. For us to enter His presence is to enter holy ground, which requires that we approach Him with the same level of holiness. This is made possible by the Holy blood of Jesus Christ.

I pray that the Holy Spirit will open your eyes to see what I have said. I pray that He will reveal Himself to you as a loving Father and seal these thoughts in the depths of your soul as He reveals this truth to you.

I mentioned earlier that God knows you intimately. He knows you much better than you know yourself. The Righteous Judge will judge your true condition and heartfelt intentions, according to His Word with complete knowledge. Be aware that the basic foundation of Salvation will not be altered or removed to fit your lifestyle or agenda.

The Bible tells us that no one mocks God:

> "Do not be deceived *and* deluded *and* misled; God will not allow Himself to be sneered at (scorned, disdained, or mocked by mere pretensions or professions, or by His precepts being set aside.) [He inevitably deludes himself who attempts to delude God.] For whatever a man sows, that *and* that only is what he will reap" (Galatians 6:7 AMP).

Be assured that we cannot mock, fool, scam, or cheat Him. Don't think you can play games with, or outwit God. We cannot even think to pretend to be saved, kill ourselves, and hope we will go to Heaven. God will not be mocked! I know this sounds harsh but if that is what it takes to shake you, then I must shake you.

The Lord, our God, despises dishonesty of heart. God knows our heart, and His justice will not allow Him to receive someone as a son or a daughter whom He knows is deceiving Him or themselves.

Once again I implore you, please wake up! Reconsider choosing suicide to resolve your problems and escape your responsibilities. It is ultimately a very selfish act, and it is the worst possible choice you could make. The Word of the Lord tells us:

"For whoever desires to save his life will lose it, but whoever loses his life for My sake and the gospel's will save it" (Mark 8:35 NKJV).

Understand that the Lord offers you eternal life, which is an opportunity to live on earth for His glory, to accomplish His purposes; and then to spend eternity in Heaven with Him when you die. He has a specific plan for you. It's not too late for you to fulfill it. God will use everything in your life, every success, every loss, every good work, every sin, every victory and every terrible episode. He will weave them together so that nothing is wasted. Eternal life will be yours the moment you make the commitment to turn from yourself and your sin;

to surrender your life to His Lordship (His purposes), and to receive Him in your heart.

God is greater than your present problems or future outcomes. He will use all your experiences as a testimony for others. (Romans 8:28) His favorite arena in which to work is called impossible. You must make the choice to trust in Him. Stop looking at everyone and everything else for a moment. Move your focus from your present circumstances to your Creator God. He rewards those who diligently seek Him.

> "But without faith it is impossible to please Him, for he who comes to God must believe that He is, and that He is a rewarder of those who diligently seek Him" (Hebrews 11:6 NKJV).

God has a plan for you from the moment you were conceived in your mother's womb. (Psalm 139) Once you receive Him as Lord of your life, He will take everything you have experienced in this life and work it together for your good. He will take all of the bad things you've done, and all of the bad things done against you and work them for your good. He will take all of your sin and shortcomings you've committed and all of your mistakes and work them together for your good. (Romans 8:28) You will then impact peoples' lives and influence them in a positive way. Do not give up!

Instead, run to God and hide in Him. Please take the time to read Psalm 91 which will tell you how to hide in God.

As I have mentioned, God knows the true intentions of our hearts. He knows us much better than we know ourselves. We may think that we are honest about something, but God can look straight into our hearts and knows when we are not honest.

Rest assured, that if you begin to contemplate ending your life, He will know it entirely. He has promised that He will always provide us a way of escaping any temptation, trial or situation we are in, and no situation will be greater than we can bear. He knows we are already capable of overcoming it. (1 Corinthians 10:13) He will judge you accordingly. Playing "Russian roulette" with your eternal destiny is not a solution to your problems. There is a tremendous likelihood you will be damned for all eternity. Wake up!

Need Help?

National Suicide Prevention Lifeline: **800.273.8255**

Christian Suicide Prevention: **888.667.5947**

SAMHSA (Substance Abuse/Mental Health): **800.662.4357** or Text **CTL** to **741741**

Chapter Thirteen
NEVER GIVE UP

I cannot tell you that I have all the answers. In fact many times I think I have more questions than answers. That's what this book is all about. My quest to find the answers as I searched my heart and God's Word. My necessity to hear God's voice, discern His ways and understand His promises. My hearts cry to know Him as my "Daddy in Heaven" and that He would be more real to me than I have ever known Him. These are all questions that he answered emphatically. I suspect that you also have doubts, regrets, and sorrows just like me.

I dare not ask you to follow my example, as recorded in this book, in relating to your children, or spouse. Each situation is unique and must be evaluated accordingly. I often wish that I had handled Jorge's life differently from the beginning. As you know, hindsight is always 20/20. It's always easy to look back, with the wisdom and understanding we have today and think how we might have handled things differently. Many times in life we simply don't have that ability or option, and in my case, I certainly don't.

Instead, all that remains are photos, videos, and memories that I pray will not vanish as time passes. I ask that my memory of the sound of my son's voice will not disappear. I hope to dream with him every night that I close my eyes.

However, one thing is for certain. I need the Lord. I need God now, more than ever. I have needed Him all my life, and

I will continue to need Him until the day I draw my final breath. I know that in Him all good things exist and outside of Him nothing of value exists. Even unseen things like the air we breathe, the love we feel, the capacity we have to laugh and rejoice, and our sense of peace, calm, and rest. He is in the light and the colors I see. He is in the beauty of nature I sense around me. I sense him in His provision for me. Above all, I have the confidence of knowing that I am deeply loved and protected by Him. Yes, protected by Him, as was my son through everything. God is faithful, and His promises are "yes" and "amen" in Jesus Christ to the glory of God Father through (to) us. (2 Corinthians 1:20)

I cannot imagine living life without Him. I need His healing when I am sick; His restoration when I am broken; His rest when I have anguish; His love when I feel abandoned; and His confidence when I doubt. I am 100% certain of my need for Him! We all do!

I love how Jesus answered His disciples once, when He said, "With man, is it impossible, but with God, all things are possible!" (Matthew 19:26) Jesus is our only hope because He is Christ in us our Hope of Glory. He is our only hope for eternal life.

There are great challenges ahead for each of us. Life is not easy. You and I have many more battles coming our way. Some may be less intense than others, but they will come. We each need a place of refuge from those storms; to know that everything will be okay, no matter what.

Through the pages of this book, you have read the agonizing story of a mother. You've seen how I desperately tried to help rescue my son from a vast array of sorrows and devastation. You have read how I sought answers in my faith, in psychological counseling, and in my core beliefs (values) on how to address the challenges that Jorge and I faced as our lives unfolded. I fought hard against much opposition to find freedom for my son, and myself.

If there is any advice that I can offer you, it is to surround yourself with Godly counsel. Seek help from your church, from Christian counseling, search God's Word, and listen to the voice of your spouse (Biblical). Don't listen to everyone. Rely only on those who are wise, discerning, and mature in the Lord. Godly pastors, mentors and experts in the areas you are experiencing will help you sort out the dysfunctions in life, and protect you from calamity in other areas of your life.

Perhaps you are wondering if I feel like a winner or a loser. I am a winner. I didn't handle every aspect of my journey perfectly, but I did so with as much integrity as I possessed. I am proud of my husband, my family, my counselors and my spiritual mentors, and myself. We operated with three strong principals: faith, values, and psychological understanding.

I am also extremely proud to see my youngest son flourishing. He is becoming an amazing and incredible man of God who was mentored by my husband and by Pastor Dr. John R. Counts. I am thrilled that my son is well and not corrupted by his late brother's misbehavior. Today I see how my husband's advice was precisely correct to bring about the best outcome. I'm satisfied knowing that I kept my faith; and learned to exercise sincere love, without compromising the truth. Even when the fight was intense, I lifted my hands to the Heavens and worshiped my Lord with sincerity of heart.

Lion's Den

Remember when the Lions Den is open, and the Lions are fast approaching, the fight is about to begin. It is those who are in Christ, those who have His blood, those who carry His name are prepared to battle the Lions. We who are in Christ have all authority, dominion and power over the kingdom of darkness. If we stand on His Word, we have nothing to fear. We are the army that's already won the war!

Understand, before we encounter our enemies on life's battlefield, we need to:

— Accept Jesus Christ as Personal Lord and Savior (He is Eternal Life)
— Be Filled and Baptized in the Holy Spirit (He Gives Us Power to Overcome in Life)
— Read God's Word/Bible (God Speaks His Wisdom, His Direction, His Encouragement to Us)
— Pray to God Only By, Through and In the Name of Jesus Christ (God Speaks His Wisdom, His Direction, His Encouragement to Us)

— Get Involved in Christian Church (Help You get Established in Faith)
— Get Baptized in Water
— Live with Attitude of Forgiveness
— Put on Helmet of Salvation (Sound Mind)
— Know God (Father, Son and Holy Spirit) Works In and Through You
— Remember Who You are in Christ, Who Christ is in You and Recognize Your Spiritual Adversaries

Trust God to use even your negative life experiences for His glory. Nothing that happens is wasted with our Lord, not a single tear.

In every area of our lives, all we need is Him. Listen to His voice and flow with His counsel. I know it is a popular Scripture, but we truly are more than conquerors in Jesus Christ. He gives us victory over sin, death, and destruction:

"So when this corruptible shall have put on incorruption, and this mortal shall have put on immortality, then shall be brought to pass the saying that is written, Death is swallowed up in victory. O death, where is thy sting? O grave, where is thy victory" (1 Corinthians 15:54-56 KJV)?

Never forget, "Everything is possible for him who believes." (Mark 9:23) Do not give up believing Him, trusting Him, relying upon Him, following Him, and loving Him. He is your best friend, partner, brother and advocate for the perfect outcome.

Long ago the Lord gave me this passage from the Book of Jeremiah that I treasure deep in my heart even today.

> "Thus says the LORD: 'Let not the wise man boast in his wisdom, let not the mighty man boast in his might, let not the rich man boast in his riches, but let him who boasts boast in this, that he understands and knows me, that I am the LORD who practices steadfast love, justice, and righteousness in the earth. For in these things I delight, declares the LORD" (Jeremiah 9:23-24 NIV).

All that I ever wanted as a mother was for my son to live here on earth with me, and not die. I wanted to share life with him by my side. A life of hugs and kisses with him, seeing his face, and hearing his laughter. A mother would never want her child to feel so depressed, alone, and hopeless that he would end his life.

I am not boasting. Even after trusting in, adhering to and relying on the Lord for so many years, my son died by his hand. Even setting aside for a moment the visions I know the

Lord deposited in my heart, I am here proclaiming faith to you. Do not tell me that you cannot believe Him. Do not tell me that your faith is weak and that you cannot overcome what you are facing today. I tell you, "Yes, you can! Yes, you can by His Spirit. Yes, you can in His strength. Yes, you can by His might. Yes, you can!"

It is my prayer, my hope, and my desire that at the end of our lives, we can proclaim these words from the apostle Paul:

> "I have fought the good fight, I have finished the race, I have kept the faith. Henceforward there is laid up for me the crown of righteousness, which the Lord, the righteous judge, will award to me on that Day, and not only to me but also to all who have loved his appearing" (2 Timothy 4:7-8 KJV).

I pray that my story, expressed in these pages, will help empower you in the name of Jesus Christ to never, never, never surrender your faith to darkness.

> "Now may the God of hope fill you with all joy and peace in believing, that you may abound in hope by the power of the Holy Spirit" (Romans 15:13 NKJV).

"Therefore we also, since we are surrounded by so great a cloud of witnesses, let us lay aside every weight, and the sin which so easily ensnares us, and let us run with endurance the race that is set before us, looking unto Jesus, the author and finisher of our faith, who for the joy that was set before Him endured the cross, despising the shame, and has sat down at the right hand of the throne of God" (Hebrews 12:1-2 NKJV).

Closing Prayer

I would like to pray for you before you finish reading this book—

"Father in Heaven, you are wonderful and powerful, forever merciful and kind. I come to you in the name of your Son and my Redeemer, Jesus Christ. I ask for your blessings and protection for the beautiful souls who are reading this book, and for each member of their family which is represented, and the circle of friends that they love. Father, perfect all the things that concern them. Prosper them, as they prosper in their faith. Equip and deliver them from the jaws of darkness. May they find strength and shelter in you. Above all, provide them with the peace that surpasses all understanding, and the wisdom to endure life's circumstances. Heal them if they are sick; save them if they are lost; restore them if they are broken, and establish them if they have lost confidence and faith. Guide them to you Lord, and give them eternal salvation. In Jesus' Name I pray. Amen."

1 John 4:4

*…He who is in you is greater than
he who is in the world.*

Appendix

How to be Born Again

By Eddie Smith

You May Need a Heart Transplant

When I was a young traveling evangelist in December 1967, on a cold Sunday night, I had finished the crusade service, enjoyed dinner, and was snuggled warmly in my motel bed watching the late evening news, when I heard a startling announcement. South African surgeon (and a preacher's son) Dr. Christiaan Barnard had performed the world's first human heart transplant. He had placed the heart of Denise Darvall, a woman in her mid-twenties, who was fatally injured in an automobile accident, inside the chest of fifty-five-year-old diabetic Louis Washkansky, who had incurable heart disease. The new heart was actually beating on its own! That, my friend, was amazing.

When the interviewer asked Dr. Barnard why he had decided to perform such a risky operation, his answer caused me to bolt upright in bed: "One look at Mr. Washkansky, and I knew he couldn't live with that old heart."

Tears immediately flooded my eyes as I realized that I too couldn't have lived with my old heart. If you've never had one, you also need a heart transplant. Not a physical heart transplant, but a spiritual one.

The Word of God tells us, "The heart is deceitful above all things, and desperately wicked" (Jeremiah 17:9). It says that "all (of us) have sinned, and come short of the glory of God" (Romans 3:23). This means that we all have "spiritual heart disease" that is always fatal, for "the wages of sin is death" (Romans 6:23). This means spiritual death, separation from God, in this life and for eternity.

We're beyond the need of CPR, or a spiritual heart massage—only a new heart will do. Everyone needs a new heart.

Good news! God loves you; He wants you to experience peace and eternal, abundant life. Today He says to you, "A new heart also will I give you... and I will take away the stony heart out of your flesh" (Ezekiel 36:26). The heavenly Father wants to perform the transplant you need.

You cannot pay for the operation because Jesus Christ has already paid the price when He died for your sins and mine on the cross. Today you can have a new heart, a clean heart, a pure heart by doing just as David the psalmist did. He asked God for it. He prayed, "Create in me a clean heart, O God" (Psalm 51: 10). And guess what-the Lord did!

God didn't create us as robots to automatically obey and serve Him. He created us in His own image and gives us freedom to choose for or against Him.

Like the first man and woman, Adam and Eve, who chose their own way in the Garden of Eden and sinned against God, we too have chosen to disobey Him and go our own way. The result is that our sin has separated us from God.

Worse still, as hard as we may try, and regardless of our good intentions, there is no way we can be reconciled to God apart from Jesus Christ. Only Christ and His cross can reconnect us to God.

Jesus died on the cross and arose from the grave in order to pay the penalty for our sin and bridge the gap between God and us.

Here then is the solution:

(1) Recognize and admit that you've sinned against God.

(2) Acknowledge that you need a Savior, that you cannot save yourself.

(3) Repent by turning from your sins.

(4) Believe in your heart that Jesus died for you and that the Father raised Him from the dead on the third day. He is alive!

(5) Now trust Jesus Christ as your personal Lord and Savior by inviting Him to live in your heart through His Holy Spirit.

Are you ready? Good!

Right now, right where you are, turn to God and say,

Dear God, I know that I have sinned against you. I am a sinner. I need your forgiveness. I need a new, clean heart. I am turning from my sins. Forgive and cleanse me. I trust you as my Savior, and give you my life. Come into my heart today, Risen Christ, and be Lord of my life. I choose to follow you. Thank you for the new life you've given me. Thank you for my new, clean heart. In Jesus' name I pray. Amen.

Did you sincerely turn to Christ? Did you invite Him into your life? Then congratulations! He has washed away your sins and now He lives in you! This is what the Scripture calls being born again, a supernatural work of God's Spirit, who is now within you.

This is the only cure for spiritual heart trouble. Now, with Jesus Christ as your Savior and with the new heart He has given you, you have everlasting life! Now you can relate to Him on a brand-new level. He is your Father, and you are his child. Best of all, when you take your last breath and pass from this physical body, you'll be present with God in heaven and will live with Him forever!

"Blessed are the pure in heart: for they shall see God" (Matthew 5:8).

"The LORD seeth not as man seeth; for man looketh on the outward appearance, but the LORD looketh on the heart" (1 Samuel 16:7).

Here are some helpful steps you can take to develop and deepen your new relationship with God.

(1) Get to know the Lord by reading your Bible every day. I suggest that you start with the New Testament book of Philippians.

(2) Converse with God continually through prayer. Talk with Him. He is your Daddy now. Tell Him how you feel, and what you need.

(3) Don't allow sins pile up and rob you of your joy. Make a practice of confessing your sins on a daily basis. Better still, the moment you commit them.

(4) Above all, listen to Him. He will speak to your heart through His Spirit.

(5) Attend a Bible-teaching church where you can worship and serve God and fellowship with other believers.

(6) Ask the pastor to baptize you, as Jesus has commanded each of us. Water baptism is a symbol of putting off your old life in sin, and putting on your new life in Christ, a picture of burial and resurrection.

(7) Share your new life with others. Invite them to do as you have done, so they too can experience God's peace and live forever with Him.

Finally, please write to the author of this book and tell her of your decision to follow Christ.

For additional information and resources,

please visit:

www.mysonkilledhimself.com

CPSIA information can be obtained
at www.ICGtesting.com
Printed in the USA
BVHW081227220419
546167BV00024B/1462/P